Towards a Professional Model
of Surrogate Motherhood

Ruth Walker · Liezl van Zyl

Towards a Professional Model of Surrogate Motherhood

palgrave
macmillan

Ruth Walker
University of Waikato
Hamilton, Waikato, New Zealand

Liezl van Zyl
University of Waikato
Hamilton, Waikato, New Zealand

ISBN 978-1-137-58657-5   ISBN 978-1-137-58658-2   (eBook)
DOI 10.1057/978-1-137-58658-2

Library of Congress Control Number: 2017937932

Cover image: © ninjaMonkeyStudio/Getty Images

Printed on acid-free paper

This Palgrave Macmillan imprint is published by Springer Nature
The registered company is Macmillan Publishers Ltd.
The registered company address is: The Campus, 4 Crinan Street, London, N1 9XW, United Kingdom

For our families

Preface

This book emerged from a puzzle we have been trying to solve for some years. Although there is growing public support for surrogacy itself, there is deep division on whether surrogates should be paid for what they do. It seemed to us to be deeply unfair to the women who act as surrogates not to compensate them in some way for their arduous undertaking. However, we could also see that there are significant problems with commercial surrogacy. Payment appears repugnant because it turns surrogacy into a business transaction. The public appears to want surrogates to have the right motives, that is, altruistic caring and selflessness, and it treats payment as a sign that they are only 'doing it for the money' or that they are selling themselves.

There is a wide diversity of views about which forms of surrogacy are acceptable and which are not. This suggests confusion among policy makers and legislators as to how best to regulate a phenomenon that has grown faster than anyone was prepared for. It also shows that a few moral issues have become the defining ones that everyone tries to solve, such as whether a woman can freely consent to bearing and relinquishing a baby in advance (that is, prior to establishing a pregnancy), whether surrogate mothers may or should be paid, whether surrogacy necessarily involves a form of objectification, and whether all or some forms of surrogacy are inherently exploitative and/or immoral. However, regardless of the regulatory framework adopted in response to these questions, moral problems persist and more are generated by each attempt to restrict surrogacy to one tightly controlled form over another.

The legal regime states adopt is partly responsible for the persistence of moral problems. The issue of legal parenthood, that is, who should be recognized as the legal parents of babies born through surrogacy, creates an ethical minefield. The decision over whether surrogacy agreements should be enforceable, or even permitted, has significant ethical ramifications. In jurisdictions where surrogacy is permitted, the issue of who should be allowed to access it has profound implications for basic human rights to freedom and equality. Many jurisdictions restrict surrogacy to heterosexual married couples who are infertile or have a medical condition that precludes pregnancy. The increasing popularity of transnational surrogacy gives rise to the question of whether children born through surrogacy abroad should have their birth and citizenship recognised by the intended parents' home state. Again, the answer states give directly impacts the baby's human rights

In some jurisdictions, including Switzerland, Finland, Iceland, France and Italy, it is illegal to enter a surrogacy agreement. The prohibition of surrogacy in these countries is typically motivated by the perceived risk of psychological or physical harm to surrogates and children born through surrogacy, as well as the view that it involves objectifying surrogates and children.

Commercial surrogacy is permitted in a small number of US States, including California, New Hampshire, and Illinois, as well as in Russia, Ukraine, and Thailand. In most of these places surrogacy agreements are enforceable. The justification typically given for this approach is that the intended parents and the surrogate have the freedom to enter a legal contract from which both parties benefit.

In many other countries, such as Canada, England, New Zealand, South Africa and Australia (except for Northern Territory), unpaid or 'altruistic' surrogacy is permitted while commercial surrogacy is prohibited. This reflects a widely held belief that while commercial surrogacy involves objectifying or commodifying babies and exploiting vulnerable women, altruistic surrogacy is motivated purely by love or kindness and involves freely giving the 'gift of life'. In most jurisdictions that only allow altruistic surrogacy, the agreement to relinquish the child is not enforceable. The surrogate and her husband/partner, if she has one, are recognised as the legal parents. She promises to allow the intended parents to adopt the child, but remains free to change her mind. Thus, one difficulty with this form of surrogacy is that legal parentage remains uncertain.

A notable exception is South Africa, where altruistic surrogacy agreements are enforceable on condition that they have been validated by the High Court prior to fertilization. This means that the intended parents will be recognized as the legal parents from the outset. This approach has the advantage of ensuring certainty over legal parentage, but it raises serious concerns about fairness: while the surrogate is required to relinquish the baby to the intended parents (and hence is not freely giving a gift), they have no obligations towards her. They are not required to give anything in return, and indeed, are legally prohibited from doing so.

We think there is an alternative to the commercial and altruistic models of surrogacy, one that recognizes the caring motives women have while at the same time compensating them for their work. The professions offer the guide we need. They provide services that are fundamentally ethical in nature, but professionals are not expected to care without compensation. Surrogates provide a service, a form of care that is inherently ethical, and should, therefore, be compensated.

The professional model needs to pass two tests. It has to have a rigorous theoretical underpinning drawn from the relevant empirical literature so that it truly reflects the way people tend to behave, the mistakes they are prone to make and how they could be effectively safeguarded. Second, it has to be practical and able to translate into a coherent, workable regulatory framework. We believe that it does pass these tests, but we present it here for readers to decide for themselves.

We were fortunate enough to receive funding from the Faculty of Arts and Social Sciences, University of Waikato, which enabled us to conduct interviews with people who have experienced surrogacy either as surrogates or as intended parents. We could not have written this book without the insight and wisdom our participants provided. Their generosity in sharing their stories with us has informed our perspective and recommendations and we are grateful to them. We also received funding for research assistance and would like to thank Stephanie Gibbons and Donya Keyhani for their invaluable help and inexhaustible patience. Heather Morell, our subject librarian, provided technical support throughout the project and crucial assistance with preparing the manuscript. We are very grateful to her. We would also like to thank the anonymous reviewers for their very helpful and constructive comments.

Hamilton, New Zealand   Ruth Walker
                                                              Liezl van Zyl

Contents

1

Three Models of Surrogacy

Introduction

We think surrogacy is a legitimate path to family formation and should be permitted for both heterosexual and same-sex couples. In this book, we set out the case for reform of the practice and argue that many of the difficulties with it arise from the ways it is currently regulated. Many of the concerns that people have about surrogacy are actually concerns about particular forms of surrogacy. We share them but argue that surrogacy could be regulated in a way that would eliminate these concerns.

It is somewhat controversial to claim that the practice of surrogacy is not in itself immoral. However, our confidence in the acceptability of surrogacy is partly based on the growing empirical research on participants in surrogacy, including intended parents, surrogates, surrogates' families and the children born from surrogacy who are now entering their teens. Ethical concerns about the practice centre on possible harms to the children born of surrogacy, the surrogates, or the other children of surrogates. Longitudinal studies show that these fears are unwarranted. The children are as well-adjusted as the children born of reproductive technologies that have become standard in fertility treatment,

© The Author(s) 2017
R. Walker and L. van Zyl, *Towards a Professional Model of Surrogate Motherhood*,
DOI 10.1057/978-1-137-58658-2_1

e.g. IVF and donor insemination (Blake et al. 2014; Bos and van Balen 2010). A large majority of surrogates relinquish the babies without difficulty and have no regrets later on, regardless of whether they were gestational or genetic surrogates (Imrie and Jadva 2014). Families created by surrogacy usually disclose this to their children, although the age at which this is done varies. They do so far more readily than families created through donor insemination where secrecy is the norm (Jadva et al. 2012; Readings et al. 2011). The other children of surrogates also tend to be well-adjusted (Jadva and Imrie 2014).

On the whole, all parties to surrogacy tend to view the experience as a positive one, a finding that has been stable over time and across cultures (Jadva et al. 2003, 2012; MacCallum et al. 2003; Papaligoura et al. 2013). Even concerns about whether a 'normal' woman would offer to be a surrogate and not be psychologically damaged by the experience have been shown to be unfounded (Imrie and Jadva 2014; Lorenceau et al. 2015).

The way surrogacy is conducted and regulated, however, is the source of ethical problems in many jurisdictions and in the rapidly expanding transnational context. Concerns arise about surrogacy regardless of the type of arrangement. It is customary to distinguish between altruistic (unpaid) and commercial (paid) surrogacy. Although there are vast differences in the ways in which both forms of surrogacy are practised and regulated in different countries, it is possible to identify a more or less coherent set of beliefs and norms that underlie these practices and regulations. We refer to these sets of beliefs and norms as 'models'. In what follows we discuss the altruistic and commercial models of surrogacy, problems with them, and our proposed alternative, the professional model.

In this chapter, we provide an overview of the dominant models of surrogacy and the moral, legal and conceptual issues that will be addressed in this book. We outline the professional model and explain how it would solve many of the problems that beset surrogacy as we currently know it. In the chapters that follow we give a detailed analysis of those problems and our proposed solutions.

The Altruistic Model

Altruistic surrogacy is uncompensated or unpaid surrogacy where the surrogate is reimbursed for direct, reasonable expenses only (Galbraith et al. 2005; Wang et al. 2016). That is common to all definitions of altruistic surrogacy. Lost earnings are sometimes treated as a legitimate expense (Hieda 2015; Peet 2016), but this is not always the case. The surrogate's motivation can be included in the definition as well. The altruistic surrogate acts from 'concern, kindness, friendship, and/or kinship' (Panitch 2013: 276). Rhonda Shaw (2008: 16) defines an altruistic act as one that 'seeks to increase or enhance another's welfare, life chances or pleasure, not one's own.' A person who acts altruistically 'expects no external reward or reciprocation.' Some scholars emphasize that it is fully voluntary and, therefore, morally acceptable (Scherman et al. 2016), and some also see it as part of a gift relationship (Fenton-Glynn 2016).

Not everyone specifies what the surrogate is giving for free but Barbara Stark (2011: 369) says 'she is not paid for her labor.' Dave Snow (2016) thinks that governments ban payment in order to prevent surrogacy from becoming an occupation. If it is unpaid it also, of course, prevents any possibility of selling babies. Altruistic surrogacy is held in high regard and is frequently the only form of surrogacy permitted. However, it gives rise to various ethical and conceptual difficulties that should make advocates cautious.

Difficulties with Altruistic Surrogacy

Altruistic surrogacy is understood in a number of different ways and these are not always consistent with each other. It is frequently described as a freely bestowed gift—the surrogate is often praised for giving 'the gift of life'. However, thinking of surrogacy as a gift from the surrogate to the intended parents also renders the surrogate vulnerable to disappointment and even emotional harm. Recipients in gift relationships are normally expected to reciprocate. It is not uncommon—or unreasonable—for a surrogate to expect something significant from the intended parents, such as having a continuing relationship with them and the child, or to be given something meaningful in the way of a thank you and acknowledgement of what she has done for them. Yet she is unlikely to state her expectations because the nature of a gift relationship is such that gifts to each other are meant to be spontaneous and freely chosen, not specified in advance. Choosing, and knowing when to bestow, appropriate gifts is part of being socially competent. However, the intended parents are unlikely to give her anything in return. This could be because they are not allowed to compensate her in any material way, or because they view her action as purely altruistic. The norms of a gift relationship are at odds with the notion of a purely altruistic action, where there is no expectation of reciprocation. Where the intended parents view (and, indeed, are encouraged to view) the surrogate's motives and actions as purely altruistic, their assumption is that she does not, and should not, expect anything in return for her selfless act. For this reason, altruistic arrangements often result in disappointment for the surrogate. This is further aggravated by the fact that surrogacy arrangements are unusual in that the gift giver or benefactor is often worse off than the beneficiary. The only sense in which a surrogate is better off tends to be that she is able to carry a baby to term and the intended parents are not.

In ordinary gift relationships, disappointment can be met by recalibrating future contributions to the relationship or even by ending it. It is usually the case that the gifts involved are commensurate. If you give someone a carefully chosen birthday present, but on your birthday you receive only a card, you can reduce your contribution the next year. Clearly, similar options are not available to the surrogate. She is not free to decide what she will give and it is impossible to scale back once she is pregnant. An abortion would never be a proportionate response. Refusing to comply with dietary and medical requirements harms the fetus, the most vulnerable party of them all. Withholding the baby is legally possible almost everywhere but both disproportionate and unjust to the baby. It also leaves her with an unwanted baby to raise or have adopted. Caring for the intended baby *in utero* and handing it over is not merely the giving of a gift but the undertaking of a significant moral responsibility to do what she has promised both for the intended baby and the intended parents.

Treating surrogacy as a gift relationship also obscures the moral responsibilities of the intended parents towards the surrogate, as well as the fact that she is entitled to care and support throughout the pregnancy and due acknowledgement of what she has done for them. She gives of herself quite literally when she carries a baby for someone, but in the altruistic model she cannot expect any form of reciprocation in case her motives become suspect. She has to do it for the right reasons and that requires selfless giving. In Chap. 3, we examine problems with the concept of altruism as well as our reasons for preferring generosity as the relevant moral quality in surrogacy.

Some would argue that the solution to the problems with altruistic surrogacy is simply to permit commercial surrogacy, where the rights and responsibilities of each party are clearly specified and surrogates are compensated for their work. Although we agree that compensation should be a component of any ethical surrogacy framework, we think that the commercial model of surrogacy is itself deeply flawed.

The Commercial Model

On the face of it, commercial surrogacy should be easier to define than altruistic surrogacy because the meaning of 'commercial' is not in dispute and we know what surrogacy is. In fact, it is complicated. As Jenni Millbank (2015: 479) points out, commercial surrogacy is defined by what it is not. The payment is not merely reimbursement of reasonable expenses. All the definitions agree on the point that the payment a surrogate receives is over and above expenses (Galbraith et al. 2005; Ramskold and Posner 2013; Scherman et al. 2016; Snow 2016). However, what counts as a reasonable expense varies. Vagueness and lack of clarity over the class of legitimate expenses creates ambiguity and uncertainty. For example, in New Zealand, where only altruistic surrogacy is permitted, the law prohibits 'giving or receiving valuable consideration' (Anderson et al. 2012: 255).

Yet difficulties also arise when authors do specify the services for which the surrogate is paid, such as carrying a fetus to term, relinquishing the baby and giving up any parental claims on it (Hammarberg et al. 2015; Peet 2016; Wilkinson 2003). It then sounds as if they are indeed selling a baby. We discuss this issue in Chap. 2. In what follows we examine the main features of commercial surrogacy contracts and the mechanisms used for establishing parental rights.

Commercial Contracts

All surrogacy arrangements, whether altruistic or commercial, can be described as contract pregnancies in the sense that there is some kind of agreement between the parties. Our focus in this section is on commercial surrogacy contracts, where the term 'contract' is used in its ordinary and legal sense. The debate in the literature mostly concerns whether these contracts should be legally enforceable and what exactly the contract establishes.

The commercial model is a wholly contractual one: In theory, the intended parents and surrogate have the right to enter into a contract and to draw up an agreement that stipulates each party's rights and obligations. The contract is complete when the surrogate relinquishes the baby (or babies, given the frequency of multiple births) to the intended parents. In reality, however, a commercial surrogacy contract is not as straightforward as this bald description suggests.

The contract establishes what the parties must do, which at its most basic level, means the payments the intended parents will make and the conditions the surrogate will meet in order to qualify for them. The conditions are negotiated and might be constrained by particular legal prohibitions but, at a minimum, the surrogate expects to be paid and the intended parents expect to receive a baby. In fact, the central assumption underpinning every contract is that the intended parents will have a baby at the end of it. The UK banned commercial surrogacy in part because they argued that a contract that did *not* require relinquishment would be absurd. It was claimed that a commercial contract inevitably commodified the baby because it had to require relinquishment in order to be complete (Fenton-Glynn 2016). We discuss such objections in Chap. 2.

Contracts and Parental Rights

Simply taking delivery of a baby, however, is not enough to establish legal parentage. In some jurisdictions, pre-birth orders can be used to give the intended parents legal parentage but, even in these cases, there has to be some formal recognition of the fact that the woman who gave birth to the baby is not its legal mother. Most jurisdictions transfer parentage after birth. The goal of the contract, then, is widely assumed to be the transfer of parental rights to the intended parents. That is what the surrogate is thought to give up when she relinquishes the baby. In short, people believe that the contract establishes who will have parental rights (Gelmann 2010; Hanna 2010; Margalit 2014). However, parental rights cannot be transferred by contract. Parentage is determined by the courts, and only the court has the right to transfer, withhold, or remove parental rights. At most, a contract can establish an intention to parent (or not to parent, in the case of the surrogate) (McLachlan and Swales 2009).

The contract is also meant to establish the conditions the surrogate must abide by during pregnancy. These range from the reasonable recommendations to all pregnant women, such as avoiding alcohol, to the onerous and invasive regarding procedures and decision-making. Intended parents often assume they have the right to make decisions about the course of the intended baby's gestation, ranging from decisions about how many embryos to transfer to whether to opt for a caesarean delivery. They also assume that they have a right to the information needed to make these decisions. The surrogate, in turn, may believe that contractual requirements can compel her to share test results and even let the intended parents decide to terminate a pregnancy for fetal abnormality against her wishes. However, regardless of what the contract states, these assumptions are mistaken. The surrogate retains all her rights to bodily integrity and confidentiality. She cannot be required to negotiate away her right to give or withhold informed consent (Drabiak-Syed 2011) and she is the patient as far as the obstetrician is concerned. All his or her professional obligations are to her alone (Chervenak and McCullough 2009). That means she cannot be compelled to undergo screening or other procedures, disclose information about the pregnancy or to have an abortion. Nor is the obstetrician permitted to disclose information to the intended parents without her consent. A contract, in short, cannot be used to override the rights of the surrogate as a person or, specifically, as a pregnant woman receiving obstetrical services. If the contract is an employment contract, as Christine Straehle (2015) argues, it should be obvious that there are significant limitations on what the intended parents can require. All employees retain their human rights and no employer could insist on the breaches of bodily integrity that intended parents often expect.

Unfortunately, in practice, many surrogates are held to contracts that precisely do breach their human rights. Clauses are used to control a surrogate's behaviour on pain of financial penalty and, even if they would not be legally enforceable, she will be left financially worse off if she refuses to do what the intended parents want. If she goes to court to have her rights upheld then she will have to pay her legal fees, which she can ill-afford. If she does not contest the clause then she misses out on the payment by refusing to comply. For example, if she is reluctant to undergo an invasive procedure, she could miss out on an extra payment of several hundred US dollars. If the intended parents decide that she is in breach of the contract, she will lose her base compensation as well and might even be expected to repay what she has already received.

Relinquishment

The contract is intended to provide certainty to the parties about duties, rights and outcomes. We have already seen that it cannot do so because its main provisions can be overridden if they conflict with human rights or the rights and duties of external agents. However, proponents of the contract model, as well as some of its critics, have raised concerns about the surrogate's commitment to relinquishment, which is made before the pregnancy is even established. The objections focus on the vulnerability of the surrogate to a change of heart because she cannot know in advance how she will feel about giving up the baby after it is born. Pregnant women are assumed to be susceptible to a natural and normal maternal bond that forms with the fetus *in utero* and becomes an overwhelming attachment when the baby is born. Versions of this objection to surrogacy are widely distributed through the literature and we will discuss it in detail in Chap. 5. It is relevant here because of the commitment a woman makes before she knows how she will feel after she gives birth. On the face of it, if a surrogate cannot make a promise in advance to relinquish the baby, she cannot enter a surrogacy contract. The goal of the contract is, after all, to deliver a baby to the intended parents. However, scholars' usual response to the objection is to modify the contractual model rather than abandon it. They look for a way to keep surrogacy contracts but also accommodate the surrogate's potential change of heart over relinquishment.

Yehezkel Margalit, who is a legal scholar with an expertise in contract law, proposes a model that would permit the renegotiation or even setting aside of contractual provisions in the event of a change of heart or extreme change in circumstances. The gestational mother would be permitted to apply for (full or partial) parental rights if she wishes to. He thinks legal parentage should be available to anyone 'who intends, wishes and agrees to become a legal parent of the child' (Margalit 2014: 456). As the child's best interests are at the forefront, he adds the constraint that 'only an individual who fulfills the needs of the child will enjoy full parental rights' (457).

It is clear that Margalit's solution introduces even more uncertainty for the intended parents than was already present in a standard contract. The goal of the contract could be partly or entirely frustrated depending on the gestational surrogate's state of mind after the birth. It is also open to the intended parents to renegotiate more favourable terms for themselves in the event of an extreme change of circumstances, which adds to the vulnerability of the surrogate rather than reducing it. He proposes the use of 'administrative mechanisms' that would provide the necessary ancillary support to the parties prior to a contract being created in order to minimize the risk of it breaking down (Margalit 2014: 464). While these are commendable, they do not address the fundamental flaw with a modified contractual model where the contract is even less binding than it was in the old model. More uncertainty is not a solution to the problem of uncertainty.

Against Commercial Contracts

We think that the commercial model is so deeply flawed that it should be replaced rather than merely modified. The underlying principle of commercial contracts is *caveat emptor* or 'let the buyer beware'. Contracting parties are expected to be alert to the risks they face from each other in the proposed transaction and ensure that they are protected from them by provisions in the contract. They are held to be acting entirely in their own interests. The contract concerns the point where their interests coincide and they both have something to gain from it. It establishes all the rights and obligations of the parties to the transaction, limited by what is legal within the jurisdiction that recognizes the contract. These limits provide some important protections to the human rights of the people entering into a contract, but lawful contractual requirements can still be demanding and exploitative of weaker parties. The latter concern has received a good deal of attention but we think that the problem goes much deeper than that. It is the application of the contract model itself to surrogacy that is wrong.

The contract model, by its nature, cannot generate the trust that is central to surrogacy relationships. Rather than speak in terms of stronger and weaker parties to a contract, we should see the vulnerability of both the surrogate and the intended parents. The intended parents have to entrust what we call the 'gestational care' of their baby to someone else. They have almost always come to surrogacy through tragedy and disappointment and have no other way of having a child of their own. For gay couples, it might be the only way they can form a family because in many jurisdictions they are not allowed to adopt. Also their social infertility is often seen as less significant than heterosexual infertility. This is a source of vulnerability. A woman is going to gestate the fetus for them and they cannot control her behaviour. The contract can stipulate that the surrogate refrain from alcohol, tobacco and drugs, but no one can force her to adhere to these requirements. They have to trust her. A contract gives them no basis for that trust. In fact, a very detailed contract could undermine trust because it demonstrates a lack of faith in the person to do the right thing.

A related point is that the course of a pregnancy is unpredictable and it is impossible to specify a provision for every contingency. This is different from the concern that a surrogate cannot know how she will feel about relinquishment. It is a universal, tangible problem: complications during pregnancy and childbirth can present any parents with decisions they did not expect and have not planned for. In surrogacy it presents three people with a crisis and only one of them, the surrogate, has the right to decide what to do.

The contract model assumes that the surrogate is entitled to act in her own interests which is true up to a point. But while there may be two parties to the contract, there are three sets of interests at stake. The intended baby has interests that are independent of those of the intended parents and the surrogate. It has an interest in not being harmed by toxins that the surrogate might ingest, which coincides with the interests of the intended parents in having a healthy baby. However, the interests of the intended baby and the intended parents do not always coincide. In the case of severe abnormality it may not be in the interests of the intended baby to be born because of the burden of suffering it will endure. But it is important to note here that one reason that the contract model fails is because it does not include the interests of the intended baby. They are subsumed under those of the intended parents, or in some cases, those of the surrogate who claims to be acting for the intended baby.

It is important to consider the intended baby's interests independently of the interests of the intended parents and the surrogate. That is because of the interests it has following birth. A newborn baby has a strong interest in being healthy. Parents and health practitioners provide healthcare to ensure that as far as possible. The right to basic health care has many justifications, which include the prevention of harm and unnecessary suffering. It also recognizes that the opportunities people have over a lifetime to pursue their goals and happiness depend to a large extent on their state of health. Illness limits freedom and imposes significant costs on a person. Steps taken for the infant protect its future abilities, whether through immunization or early interventions to reduce the risk of chronic disease later in life, such as diabetes and heart disease.

By the time the baby is born much has already happened to raise or lower the risk of chronic disease. Exposure to toxins, such as alcohol and tobacco, can have subtle effects that can change the trajectory of the baby's life course even if it is not enough to cause fetal alcohol syndrome. What happens *in utero* cannot be entirely undone by good care after birth. If we consider the baby's interests from the baby's perspective, which includes the prospects for the whole of its life course, not just the time it is in the care of its parents, then the antenatal period must be included. That is why we make the independent consideration of the intended baby's interests a central feature the professional model. We say more about this in Chap. 5.

At the stage where a dispute arises, the contract model offers only an adversarial system. Even if court can be avoided through the use of a mediation service, the system is designed for broken relationships and lack of trust rather than for a genuinely cooperative approach to problems where both sides trust and respect each other. When these difficulties are considered alongside the fact that a contract cannot provide certainty on the matter at the heart of the arrangement—a baby recognized as the child of the intended parents—we think a different approach is needed.

The Professional Model

The literature presents us with a dichotomy: altruistic surrogacy or commercial surrogacy. We argue that it is a false dichotomy, and that there is a third alternative. A core assumption underlying the dichotomy is that unpaid surrogates are motivated by altruism, whereas commercial surrogates are motivated by money. This assumption is mistaken. Payment to the surrogate does not preclude 'altruistic' motivation. There are many professions that are worthwhile in themselves and that attract people who want to work for the good of others. Indeed, they are jobs that can only be done well when practitioners are so motivated. Specifically, they are the caring professions.

We restrict the professional model to the caring professions because, as we will show, they are the ones to which surrogacy is most analogous. Alternative models of the professions do exist but they do not focus specifically on care so are less helpful to the analysis of surrogacy. For example, we do not include law or accountancy in our analysis even though they are professions and share many features with the caring professions. There are strong ethical requirements relating to the provision of their services but they do not provide care.

Consider, then, nursing, teaching, social work, medicine and child care. People who care about their patients, students and clients will do a better a job than those who do not. The fact that they are paid does not make us say they are only in it for the money. Most people cannot afford to work unpaid and their motivation is judged by other criteria. We think surrogates should be treated the same way and that the professional model of surrogacy provides a solution to the problems that plague both altruistic and commercial surrogacy.

It is important to note at the outset that we are not advocating that surrogacy become a career. There are very good reasons for limiting the number of pregnancies a woman has and we would be concerned to see our model taken as legitimizing unlimited pregnancies that eventually put the woman's health in jeopardy. The professional model identifies what we believe to be the most useful attitude towards the practice of surrogacy and its regulation. It adapts ideals and values from the caring professions and applies them to surrogacy. A second point is that when we talk about care, we are not talking about an emotion or feeling, such as love or sympathy. We do not expect any professional to have warm feelings towards all clients at all times. Care is what they provide to clients rather than what they feel about them. We expect professionals to develop the ability to provide care in a timely manner, to a consistent standard and that is appropriate to the given needs of the recipient. Ideally, no professional feels positively uncaring but all professionals have good and bad days. What we expect is for them to hide any negative feelings in the course of their care. However, there is a third concern that might be raised: all the occupations traditionally regarded as professions require extensive training and education but surrogacy does not appear to need any training. While we acknowledge that pregnant women do not need degrees in pregnancy-related subjects, managing a surrogate pregnancy well is far from an unskilled enterprise. We think good surrogates can be distinguished from bad ones on recognizably professional lines.

Professional Norms

The distinction between professions and other occupations has always been fluid and some traditional criteria have become irrelevant. For example, instead of being paid a fee by individual clients, some professions, such as medicine, now have large numbers of salaried members. This means that some occupations, such as teaching, are now included as professions where previously they were considered to be semi-professions. However, there are distinct norms that we think are fundamental to the professions and that should be applied to surrogacy.

The first is that the professions replace the commercial principle *caveat emptor* with *primum non nocere*, 'first do no harm'. In this model, the trustworthiness of the professional is central. The professionals are trusted to put clients' interests ahead of their own. The domains of the professions are significant, and include health, education and law. All these fields concern fundamental human rights that are strong factors in human wellbeing, which means that the people they serve tend to be vulnerable in some important respect. Without access to medical care, people cannot flourish. Their life chances are determined to a large extent by their education or lack of it and, without an independent legal profession, individuals' rights to liberty, property, privacy and freedom of speech are in jeopardy should the state decide to move against them. The people in need of professional services are usually in no position to bargain for them even if they have the expertise to do it. They have to trust the professional and the professional has to be trustworthy. As a result, there is an ethical dimension to the professions that is not necessarily present in other occupations (Carr 1999). Consider again the principle 'let the buyer beware.' It applies in situations where it is reasonable to assume that the buyer can take steps to protect him or herself. When choosing a plumber or builder it is possible for the consumer to assess the competence of the tradesperson through simple research, reviews and recommendations. The jobs that they do are less complex and more standardized than those of the caring professions. It is possible to acquire enough information to make an informed decision. Similarly, purchasing products can be done with the aid of independent consumer information. Less trust is required and the consumer is less vulnerable than patients, clients and students.

To ensure that the professions are trustworthy they are structured rather differently from ordinary commercial enterprises. There is an obligatory code of ethics, legally authorized regulatory bodies to determine training, maintain ethical standards, adjudicate complaints and sanction wrongdoers. It is not enough that students intending to practice have the required technical expertise, they must also adhere to the ethical values and standards of the profession. That means selecting students for more than just academic ability. They must be receptive to the ethical education they receive and willing to apply it in their practice.

The needs of clients are complex and often unpredictable. Because the professions are founded on trust, these needs can be addressed as they occur, however unexpected they are. Both parties go into the relationship knowing that it is open-ended and will not be jeopardized in the way a contractual relationship would be.

Trust does not magically appear. Daryl Koehn (1994) argues that it is the public pledge that professionals make that grounds the trust the client can have in them. It does not guarantee that an individual practitioner will be trustworthy, but the fact that the regulatory body can remove someone from the register so that they cannot practice—and will do so—acts as an incentive to keep the rules. The public has reason to think that registered practitioners are trustworthy in a way that they do not with ordinary commercial traders and service providers.

The commercial model of surrogacy does not even pretend to establish a trusting relationship between the surrogate and intended parents. Trust can hardly be a contractual stipulation and it is the contract that determines what can be required. The altruistic model, on the other hand, assumes that the intended parents and surrogate will trust each other because the basis of the relationship is the bond they form. This bond is supposed to see them through all the possible difficulties that occur along the way, although this is scarcely realistic. Given that agreements are rarely enforceable and the consent of the birth mother is required for the transfer of parentage, the fragility of the bond should be a serious worry to advocates of altruistic surrogacy arrangements. The whole edifice depends on trust but there is no plausible mechanism for generating it. The surrogate cannot even be sure that the intended parents will agree to take the baby. If their circumstances change or there is something wrong with the baby or even if there are too many babies, they are free to walk away.

Intended parents have to find their own surrogate in altruistic surrogacy. In commercial surrogacy they might choose from a selection provided by a commercial agency or find someone for themselves who is willing to be their surrogate for the price they are offering. In both altruistic and commercial arrangements, the surrogate is an unknown quantity in many crucial respects. The intended parents tend to be looking for someone whose values are a good fit with their own and someone they can bond with. Values are difficult qualities to detect. A bond can be a superficial attraction that both parties have an unconscious interest in exaggerating. That is likely to lead to the attribution of common values where these might not exist. Once a pregnancy is established, it is too late to find out that the intended parents and surrogate have a vital difference in values. Although the success rate in surrogacy is very high if measured by relinquishment rates, this is not the same as a result that leaves both parties happy at the end of it.

The Structure of the Professional Model

The professional model seeks to minimize the risks to surrogates and intended parents. It also ensures that the intended baby's interests are represented as these are independent of the intended parents' and the surrogate's interests. It recognizes that forming a family is, for many people, a significant constituent of their happiness and that their vulnerability because of the difficulty in doing so is similarly significant. The professional model has the following features.

At the top, there is an independent regulatory body with the same functions as other professional bodies. It is responsible for licensing fertility clinics, registering surrogates, setting fees, maintaining ethical standards and monitoring compliance. It also hears complaints and has the power to discipline members, including the authority to remove registration or licenses. We explore each of these functions to show how it works to make surrogacy safer for all parties.

Licensing

Fertility clinics that offer surrogacy services are already licensed in the sense that their medical staff are registered and allowed to practise in their chosen field. Our proposal merely extends that to make surrogacy a specific service with additional requirements to ensure the protection of intended parents and surrogates. We think that all surrogacy arrangements, including traditional surrogacy, where the surrogate's eggs are used, should be under the auspices of the regulatory body to minimize risks and that the most logical place for them is the clinic, which already has some support services in place.

Clinic staff would have to abide by a code of ethics and use only registered surrogates. The regulatory body would maintain a register of women who were willing to act as surrogates and who met the relevant criteria. In current models, surrogates are screened for medical and psychological health, age, and freedom from coercion (including coercively severe financial distress). They have to be able to give informed consent. However, the assessment of values and ethical standards is not usually part of the process. In fact, in commercial agencies, they are encouraged to downplay some of their real financial motivation and sell the intended parents the idea that they are primarily motivated by a desire to help, whether they are or not (Rudrappa and Collins 2015; Karandikar et al. 2014). Elly Teman (2008) observes that researchers also tend to look for more acceptable motives in surrogates, perhaps because of their ambivalence about the morality of surrogacy. Intended parents might look for shared personal values but there is no concept of professional morality to rely on.

Registration

A registered surrogate in our model would promise to put the interests of the intended baby and intended parents ahead of her own (in the sense of the professional commitment to do so), and conduct herself ethically. She would understand that she would not be the legal mother of the baby at any stage. As things stand in most jurisdictions, the intended parents cannot hold the surrogate to her promise to relinquish the baby. We advocate a change in the way parentage is determined so that from birth, the intended parents are automatically the baby's legal parents and no transfer is necessary. The surrogate does not make a promise to relinquish the baby because it is not hers to relinquish. (These matters are discussed in detail in Chap. 5.)

The requirement to use only registered surrogates does not rule out intended parents finding their own candidates. However, it does prevent coercion of family members or friends because the regulatory body would still need to register that person. In the course of confidential interviews, they could discover that the woman feels pressured into offering and would rather not do it. In that case, a letter declining to register her would be sent to the woman and intended parents. Because the process must be confidential, no reason for refusing to register a woman would be disclosed, thus providing her with the protection she needs in order to be honest. It is just as important to protect the interests of surrogates and potential surrogates as it is to assist intended parents.

It is also important that intended parents and surrogates feel that they are a good fit for each other. With the protection of the register, both parties are in a better position to make a decision based on personal preferences. The intended parents can be confident about the ethical standards of the surrogate, and there is a reciprocal process for the intended parents who must understand and accept their responsibilities towards the surrogate before they can proceed.

Fees

The regulatory body also sets the fees for surrogates. In some jurisdictions there are limits on what professionals are allowed to charge clients. Excessive charges can be the subject of a complaint. We think that surrogacy should be no different. There would be a set fee that is fair compensation for the surrogate and not subject to bargaining. The way it is paid is also important. Commercial contracts are paid on completion, with part payments on the way. We think this is unfair to the surrogate and leads to abuses by the intended parents as well as penalizing surrogates whose pregnancies fail for some reason or who put themselves at undue risk to take a pregnancy to term because they will lose the money if they do not. Instead, we think the surrogate should receive payment in only two instalments. For the period in which the pregnancy is established and up to the end of the twelfth week, she receives half the fee. This is because miscarriage is more likely in the first trimester. But if she loses the pregnancy after that she would receive the entire amount. She is not being paid for a successful outcome, just for the time and work that goes into it. She is not in a position to guarantee a successful outcome so it would be unfair to reward her for achieving one or penalize her for not doing so. Trust accounts and insurance, paid for by the intended parents, would be obligatory.

Support Services

At no time during the pregnancy or afterwards would the surrogates and parents be without access to all the professional support services they need from medical to counselling and social workers. After the birth, there would always be follow-up services available to surrogates and parents to ensure that the transition is successful. Surrogates are often left to manage by themselves once the transfer has been completed. While they almost never regret relinquishing the baby, they often feel unsupported and struggle to adjust. Even though they have not taken the baby home, they have given birth with all the physical and emotional effects that can bring. Registered surrogates should be able to access whatever help they need very easily.

Protection for Surrogates

A final advantage of the professional model is that it can protect the surrogate from unethical demands. An often overlooked feature of regulated professions is their ability to protect individual members from demands that breach their ethical standards. Medical and nursing staff are frequently pressured by management to work dangerously long shifts or on understaffed wards both of which put patients at risk, as well as the staff. Teachers are subject to political interference driven by populism or fads that have no pedagogical value. Individual doctors, nurses and teachers can do little to resist, but their professional bodies can and do take action to protect professional standards. Surrogates come under enormous pressure to agree to practices that may not be illegal but are certainly discouraged. For example, multiple embryo transfers are used to raise the success rate of IVF, fetal reduction may then be used if too many of the embryos implant, although intended parents often want twins so that their costs are minimized. These practices not only put the surrogate at risk, they are also not in the interests of the intended baby or babies. Multiple births are more likely to result in prematurity, low birthweight, higher rates of disability and higher mortality rates (Bergh and Wennerholm 2012; Van Heesch et al. 2014).

As a condition of licensing, clinics would adopt best practice, including single embryo transfer (Wang et al. 2016). Unless there is a compelling clinical reason for transferring two embryos, single embryo transfer should be standard. The intended parents would not be able to demand more and could not provide additional financial incentives as they can in commercial surrogacy. The clinics could not pressure surrogates into doing anything unethical without putting their licence at risk. Surrogates could refuse anything that was unethical or illegal and have confidence that the regulatory body, their professional body, would support them. Professional associations that have legal standing can put the brakes on in otherwise unfettered markets, where everything is permitted unless explicitly prohibited.

Intended Parents' Responsibilities

This leads us to the responsibilities of the intended parents. Just as patients cannot demand, for any price, that doctors prescribe illegally or clients that lawyers ignore perjury, the intended parents could not require a surrogate to waive her human rights, endanger the welfare of the intended baby in the interests of economy (two for the price of one) or breach ethical standards. They would have obligations to her, which they would have to accept. The screening of intended parents is a vexed issue that we address in Chap. 6, but they must be prepared to accept their responsibilities towards the surrogate in addition to being screened for suitability as parents. The clinics could and should turn them down as patients if they are not willing to do so.

To summarize then, the professional model has the following features:

1. The surrogate is paid for her service (and not the baby).
2. The intended parents have the rights and obligations of legal parentage from the birth of the baby.
3. The regulatory framework emphasizes support for all parties, including care for the surrogate after she has given birth.
4. The surrogate cannot contract out of her rights as a pregnant woman. The intended parents must understand and respect her rights and their duties towards her.
5. Surrogates and clinics must be licensed and registered by an independent regulatory body with responsibility for ensuring that the legal and ethical standards are met.

The most significant benefit of the professional model is that it removes the prolonged uncertainty that intended parents have to endure in most countries that even allow surrogacy. This occurs because legal parentage has to be established in a stressful and expensive process that requires the cooperation not only of the surrogate and her partner, but also of the courts. It seems to be extraordinarily difficult for the public and the judiciary to accept what the intended parents and surrogate firmly believe: they are the parents, the surrogate is not. In most cases the surrogate does not want to be the parent, but, at any time, for example if the relationship comes under strain, she can threaten to withhold the baby even if she herself does not want to raise it. There is nothing the parents can do to stop her. The ordinary uncertainties around the success of IVF and carrying a healthy baby to term are compounded by the additional stress caused by the simple fact that the surrogate can hold the baby hostage. In some states in the US, genetic parentage is recognized, but that is no help to the intended mother if she is not the genetic mother of the baby and it does not prevent the surrogate shifting to a state that does not recognize the genetic mother's status.

There is also evidence of distress for the surrogates themselves in relationships that are deeply ambiguous. In studies published from 2010 to 2016, Zsuzsa Berend documents not only the sadness of US surrogates when they lose a pregnancy but also when they lose the friendship they thought they had with the intended parents after they have given them the baby. Surrogates are encouraged to focus on the selflessness of their gift to the couple. Nevertheless, from their perspective there appears to be a real bond with the intended parents during the pregnancy and an expectation of a continuing relationship.

In this regard, Joshua Shaw (2016) makes a useful distinction between what is owed to a gestational surrogate and what she deserves. Although a contract sets out what she is owed (financially, etc.), she may deserve something over and above that. It is important to acknowledge the fact that the surrogate is a person who has made it possible for the family to exist. To treat her as disposable is wrong. The professional model requires the intended parents to treat the surrogate with respect and consideration. Although we do not think she deserves a 'parent-like voice', as Shaw suggests, we think she deserves a continuing presence in the story of the family and some level of contact if she wants it. Teman (2010) describes the disposal of surrogates in Israel when they have given birth. The institutions work to keep the intended parents and the surrogate apart and it takes gumption on the part of the parents to stand up to the officials—if they are not willing collaborators in the erasure of the surrogate from the story. It is possible to overemphasize the intended mother as the real mother and impose a cost on the surrogate that she does not deserve.

Professionalism has its dangers. All too often occupations strive to be recognized as professions because of the higher status it brings and the price premium it can yield. The power to self-regulate rather than be subject to external constraints is also attractive. These are risks associated with professional status generally, which means that practitioners and the public need to be vigilant. We draw on the ideals underpinning the professions but remain mindful of the threats to those ideals.

Conclusion

Surrogacy itself is an acceptable way to form a family. The way it is currently regulated creates serious ethical problems that lead to calls to ban surrogacy altogether. At present there are two different approaches to regulation, what we term the altruistic model and the commercial model. Where the altruistic model operates surrogates are not paid and their act is seen as a gift. Under the commercial model the surrogate is paid and the entire arrangement is governed by a negotiated contract. The altruistic model is seen as preventing the sale of babies and ensuring that women are not motivated by financial gain but by a desire to help someone. The flawed assumption is that payment precludes women acting for morally good reasons. By contrast, the commercial model provides for payment but relies on a contract to stipulate all the conditions, rights and duties of both parties to it. Some of these, particularly legal parentage, cannot be established by contract. Many contracts breach the rights of the surrogate by requiring her to give decision-making power to the intended parents. Contracts cannot generate trust, which is necessary in a surrogacy relationship because pregnancy is subject to events that cannot be predicted in advance or fully specified in a contract.

We proposed the professional model as an alternative. The professional model would regulate surrogacy using the structure, values and ethical principles that underpin the caring professions such as nursing. The surrogates are paid, the intended parents have legal parentage from birth and there is a regulatory framework to uphold the rights of all parties. Clinics are licensed and surrogates are registered to ensure that ethical standards are met and that surrogates are protected from unreasonable demands. It recognizes the uncertainties that accompany pregnancy and childbirth and provides a basis for trust between intended parents and surrogate.

The professional model must take account of two very serious objections to surrogacy: that it is inherently exploitative of the surrogate and/or treats her and the baby as commodities. These are the most widely held concerns about surrogacy and we turn now to address them.

References

Anderson, L., Snelling, J., & Tomlins-Jahnke, H. (2012). The practice of surrogacy in New Zealand. *Australian and New Zealand Journal of Obstetrics and Gynaecology, 52*(3), 253–257.

Berend, Z. (2010). Surrogate losses. *Medical Anthropology Quarterly, 24*(2), 240–262.

Berend, Z. (2016). "We are all carrying someone else's child!": Relatedness and relationships in third-party reproduction. *American Anthropologist, 118*(1), 24–36.

Bergh, C., & Wennerholm, U.-B. (2012). Obstetric outcome and long-term follow up of children conceived through assisted reproduction. *Best Practice & Research Clinical Obstetrics & Gynaecology, 26*(6), 841–852.

Blake, L., Richards, M., & Golombok, S. (2014). The families of assisted reproduction and adoption. In F. Baylis & C. McLeod (Eds.), *Family-making: Contemporary ethical challenges* (pp. 64–85). Oxford: Oxford University Press.

Bos, H., & van Balen, F. (2010). Children of the new reproductive technologies: Social and genetic parenthood. *Patient Education and Counseling, 81*(3), 429–435.

Carr, D. (1999). Professional education and professional ethics. *Journal of Applied Philosophy, 16*(1), 33–46.

Chervenak, F. A., & McCullough, L. B. (2009). How should the obstetrician respond to surrogate pregnancy? *Ultrasound in Obstetrics and Gynecology, 33*(2), 131–132.

Drabiak-Syed, K. (2011). Currents in contemporary bioethics: Waiving informed consent to prenatal screening and diagnosis? Problems with paradoxical negotiation in surrogacy contracts. *Journal of Law, Medicine & Ethics, 39*(3), 559–564.

Fenton-Glynn, C. (2016). Outsourcing ethical dilemmas: Regulating international surrogacy arrangements. *Medical Law Review, 24*(1), 59–75.

Galbraith, M., McLachlan, H. V., & Swales, J. K. (2005). Commercial agencies and surrogate motherhood: A transaction cost approach. *Health Care Analysis, 13*(1), 11–31.

Gelmann, E. (2010). I'm just the oven, it's totally their bun: The power and necessity of the federal government to regulate commercial gestational surrogacy arrangements and protect the legal rights of intended parents. *Women's Rights Law Reporter, 32*, 159–192.

Hammarberg, K., Stafford-Bell, M., & Everingham, S. (2015). Intended parents' motivations and information and support needs when seeking extraterritorial compensated surrogacy. *Reproductive BioMedicine Online, 31*(5), 689–696.

Hanna, J. K. M. (2010). Revisiting child-based objections to commercial surrogacy. *Bioethics, 24*(7), 341–347.

Hieda, M. (2015). The surrogacy trail. In M. Cooper, K. Vafadari, & M. Hieda (Eds.), *Current issues and emerging trends in medical tourism* (pp. 139–152). Medical Information Science Reference: Hershey.

Imrie, S., & Jadva, V. (2014). The long-term experiences of surrogates: Relationships and contact with surrogacy families in genetic and gestational surrogacy arrangements. *Reproductive Biomedicine Online, 29*(4), 424–435.

Jadva, V., Blake, L., Casey, P., & Golombok, S. (2012). Surrogacy families 10 years on: Relationship with the surrogate, decisions over disclosure and children's understanding of their surrogacy origins. *Human Reproduction, 27*(10), 3008–3014.

Jadva, V., & Imrie, S. (2014). Children of surrogate mothers: Psychological well-being, family relationships and experiences of surrogacy. *Human Reproduction, 29*(1), 90–96.

Jadva, V., Murray, C., Lycett, E., MacCallum, F., & Golombok, S. (2003). Surrogacy: The experiences of surrogate mothers. *Human Reproduction, 18*(10), 2196–2204.

Karandikar, S., Gezinski, L. B., Carter, J. R., & Kaloga, M. (2014). Economic necessity or noble cause? A qualitative study exploring motivations for gestational surrogacy in Gujarat, India. *Affilia, 29*(2), 224–236.

Koehn, D. (1994). *The ground of professional ethics*. New York: Routledge.

Lorenceau, E. S., Mazzucca, L., Tisseron, S., & Pizitz, T. D. (2015). A cross-cultural study on surrogate mother's empathy and maternal–foetal attachment. *Women and Birth, 28,* 154–159.

MacCallum, F., Lycett, E., Murray, C., Jadva, V., & Golombok, S. (2003). Surrogacy: The experience of commissioning couples. *Human Reproduction, 18*(6), 1334–1342.

Margalit, Y. (2014). In defense of surrogacy agreements: A modern contract law perspective. *William & Mary Journal of Women and the Law, 20*(2), 423–468.

McLachlan, H. V., & Swales, J. K. (2009). Commercial surrogate motherhood and the alleged commodification of children: A defense of legally enforceable contracts. *Law and Contemporary Problems, 72*(3), 91–107.

Millbank, J. (2015). Rethinking 'commercial' surrogacy in Australia. *Journal of Bioethical Inquiry, 12*(3), 477–490.

Panitch, V. (2013). Surrogate tourism and reproductive rights. *Hypatia, 28*(2), 274–289.

Papaligoura, Z., Papadatou, D., & Bellali, T. (2013). The experiences of Greek individuals in families created through gestational surrogacy arrangements: A preliminary study. In *Human Reproduction* (pp. 275–275). Oxford: Oxford University Press.

Peet, J. L. (2016). A womb that is (not always) one's own. *International Feminist Journal of Politics, 18*(2), 1–19.

Ramskold, L. A. H., & Posner, M. P. (2013). Commercial surrogacy: How provisions of monetary remuneration and powers of international law can prevent exploitation of gestational surrogates. *Journal of Medical Ethics, 39*(6), 397–402.

Readings, J., Blake, L., Casey, P., Jadva, V., & Golombok, S. (2011). Secrecy, disclosure and everything in-between: Decisions of parents of children conceived by donor insemination, egg donation and surrogacy. *Reproductive BioMedicine Online, 22*(5), 485–495.

Rudrappa, S., & Collins, C. (2015). Altruistic agencies and compassionate consumers: Moral framing of transnational surrogacy. *Gender & Society, 29*(6), 937–959.

Scherman, R., Misca, G., Rotabi, K., & Selman, P. (2016). Global commercial surrogacy and international adoption: Parallels and differences. *Adoption & Fostering, 40*(1), 20–35.

Shaw, J. (2016). What do gestational mothers deserve? *Ethical Theory and Moral Practice, 19*(4), 1031–1045.

Shaw, R. (2008). Rethinking reproductive gifts as body projects. *Sociology, 42*(1), 11–28.

Snow, D. (2016). Criminalising commercial surrogacy in Canada and Australia: The political construction of 'national consensus'. *Australian Journal of Political Science, 51*(1), 1–16.

Stark, B. (2011). Transnational surrogacy and international human rights law. *ILSA Journal of International & Comparative Law, 18*(2), 369–386.

Straehle, C. (2015). Is there a right to surrogacy? *Journal of Applied Philosophy, 33*(2), 146–159.

Teman, E. (2008). The social construction of surrogacy research: An anthropological critique of the psychosocial scholarship on surrogate motherhood. *Social Science and Medicine, 67*(7), 1104–1112.

Teman, E. (2010). *Birthing a mother: The surrogate body and the pregnant self.* Berkeley: University of California Press.

Van Heesch, M. M. J., Evers, J. L. H., Dumoulin, J. C. M., et al. (2014). A comparison of perinatal outcomes in singletons and multiples born after in vitro fertilization or intracytoplasmic sperm injection stratified for neonatal risk criteria. *Acta Obstetricia et Gynecologica Scandinavica, 93*(3), 277–286.

Wang, A. Y., Dill, S. K., Bowman, M., & Sullivan, E. A. (2016). Gestational surrogacy in Australia 2004–2011: Treatment, pregnancy and birth outcomes. *Australian and New Zealand Journal of Obstetrics and Gynaecology, 56*(3), 255–259.

Wilkinson, S. (2003). The exploitation argument against commercial surrogacy. *Bioethics, 17*(2), 169–187.

2

Exploitation and Commodification

Introduction

The biggest concern that people have about surrogacy is that, however it is organized, the practice itself is inherently exploitative of women and turns them, their bodies and the babies into commodities. No model of surrogacy could work if exploitation and commodification are the inevitable results of allowing women to carry babies for others. To determine whether surrogacy exploits women and turns them into commodities, it is important to be clear about what these terms mean. In the first part of this chapter, we look closely at the concept of exploitation. It is not immediately obvious what makes a practice exploitative. What often comes to mind when people worry about surrogacy is its similarity to sweated labour, which is exploitative. But what makes it exploitative? Is it the low pay, the bad conditions or the lack of alternatives for impoverished workers? These features tend to occur together, but do they have to in order for it to be exploitation? What if workers choose to work in those settings because they are better off than they would be in any of the meagre alternatives? Is exploitation ever acceptable? The answers to all these questions are complex and still much debated, even in the case

© The Author(s) 2017   **29**
R. Walker and L. van Zyl, *Towards a Professional Model of Surrogate Motherhood*,
DOI 10.1057/978-1-137-58658-2_2

of sweated labour. In surrogacy, they have only begun to be addressed. Commodification is a separate issue that we discuss in the second part of this chapter. We will show that both objections apply to some aspects of contemporary surrogacy but argue that it need not be exploitative. Reforms can also remove the elements of commodification that are so often present, especially in transnational surrogacy. The professional model is specifically designed to prevent the exploitation of women and all forms of commodification.

Exploitation

Our first task is to define exploitation. Our discussion focuses on transnational surrogacy because it causes the gravest concerns about exploitation. However, the account of exploitation presented in this chapter can be applied to all surrogacy arrangements. Exploitation occurs in transactions between people. We will use a hypothetical set of intended parents and surrogate to explain the concept and explore the relevant nuances.

The Allbrights would like Bandini to act as their surrogate. The Allbrights are wealthy and Bandini is poor, and the Allbrights have chosen transnational surrogacy mainly because it is less expensive than domestic surrogacy. Bandini will not receive nearly as much as a surrogate in their home country would. She has little bargaining power and few options for improving her situation. Are the Allbrights exploiting her? That depends on whether the Allbrights are taking unfair advantage of Bandini. We will consider only scenarios where both parties benefit from the arrangement. If the Allbrights' share of that benefit is excessive compared with Bandini's, then they are taking unfair advantage of her and exploiting her. However, even if they are taking unfair advantage of her, Bandini could be better off as a result of being a surrogate for the Allbrights than she would have been from any of the alternative options available to her. Alan Wertheimer (1996: 16–21) refers to this as 'mutually advantageous exploitation'. That is, Bandini is better off as a result of entering the arrangement with the Allbrights but she does not receive as much from it as she should. This form of exploitation could be justifiable. We address the issue of justification further on in the chapter, but it is important to make the point that exploitation can sometimes be justified. However, before we can assess whether it is acceptable to exploit Bandini, we have to have a way of determining whether the Allbrights are taking unfair advantage of her. To do this, we examine the price being offered and how the benefits are distributed.

Unfair Advantage

The Allbrights would have a maximum price that they were prepared to pay and Bandini would have a minimum price that she would accept. If the Allbrights managed to pay a lot less than their maximum, somewhere close to Bandini's minimum, they would receive a far bigger share of the benefit arising from the transaction and would gain it at her expense. If, by contrast, they paid a price somewhat lower than their maximum but somewhat higher than Bandini's minimum, then she would receive a fair share of the benefit generated by the transaction. For example, she might be lifted out of poverty instead of left financially precarious. Only then could we say that she had received fair payment and not been exploited. Yet, it could still make sense for Bandini to be their surrogate even if she is exploited, as long as she gains some benefit that she would not have had otherwise. It does not make the arrangement fair, it just means that it is rational of Bandini to agree to it. That is what makes mutually advantageous exploitation morally complicated, as we will show.

There is another way of looking at the Allbrights' wrongful gain at Bandini's expense. Although it is true that, in absolute terms, she is better off being their surrogate, she is not as well off as she would have been if the transaction had been fair. She has suffered an undeserved loss relative to what she would have received if the transaction had been fair (Mayer 2007b). Bandini is in a position analogous to that of sweatshop labourers whose exploiter does not benefit them enough (Mayer 2007b: 142).

Regardless of whether we interpret Bandini's loss in absolute or relative terms, the problem with transactions like these is that the benefits are distributed unjustly. The weaker party, in our case Bandini, does not receive her fair share.

Invalid Consent

Not everyone agrees that the unfair (unjust) distribution of benefits is enough by itself to count as exploitation. Stephen Wilkinson (2015, 2003a, b) calls that the 'disparity of value' condition but adds that Bandini's consent to the arrangement would also have to be invalid in order for us to say that the Allbrights had exploited her. Wilkinson argues that it is invalid consent that turns unfairness into exploitation because unfair distributions can be caused by 'bad luck' or 'negligence' or even generosity on the part of the disadvantaged party, a point we discuss in Chap. 3, but if there is valid consent it is not exploitation (Wilkinson 2015: 4). It is certainly important that Bandini gives her consent to the arrangement but it is not obvious why the Allbrights would escape the charge of exploitation just because she does so.

We think that Wilkinson adds the consent condition because of the way he regards altruistic surrogacy. Altruistic surrogacy is unpaid, and Wilkinson holds that it is not exploitative. On the contrary, he thinks it is ideal. This creates a problem for him. If we apply the 'disparity of value' test, then altruistic surrogacy emerges as the most exploitative of all surrogacy arrangements. Even the most unfairly paid commercial arrangement is less exploitative than one where the surrogate gets nothing. In order to avoid this conclusion, Wilkinson adds a second requirement: there must also be invalid consent.

Wilkinson would agree that it could be rational for Bandini to give consent to an unjust arrangement. In cases of mutually advantageous exploitation, it could make more sense for her to consent than to refuse. She will get some benefit and be better off in absolute terms. In order for her to give informed consent, she has to be competent, that is able to make decisions for herself, have enough information and be free from coercion. No one is allowed to pressure her into consenting. If she is given all the information about the surrogacy in her own language, has a copy of the contract and understands what is in it, then the only real concern is whether she is being coerced.

If the Allbrights or the clinic they are using, or Bandini's husband were threatening her into agreeing, then that would be a very obvious case of coercion. But Wilkinson (2015) argues that there are other ways in which someone can be coerced. Bandini is poor and has few options because she lives in a poor country. These are her background conditions. If these conditions are caused by the actions of others or their failure to do something they should, for example poverty alleviation, then the conditions are themselves coercive and Bandini cannot freely consent to be the Allbrights' surrogate. It is not simply the fact that Bandini has few alternatives to surrogacy that makes her consent invalid. A lack of alternatives by itself does not invalidate consent. Quite ordinary situations requiring consent have no alternatives. Wilkinson suggests life-saving medical treatment but, much less dramatically in medical contexts, there is frequently only one treatment for a condition. Consent to a course of antibiotics for a 'strep throat' is not invalidated just because there are no other treatments and to leave it untreated would be risky.

On the face of it, the addition of the consent condition is plausible. Wilkinson compares a wealthy person volunteering to work for unfairly low pay to a poor person forced into working for unfairly low pay because his lack of alternatives is due to others' neglect of their duties towards him. Consent is indeed the crucial distinction in that example. However, the consent condition also leads to some less plausible outcomes. If a poor person is not coerced into working for unfairly low pay and gives valid consent, we are required to say that she is not exploited regardless of how unfairly low her share of the benefits is. This seems quite an odd conclusion. What goes wrong?

We think that Wilkinson is right to avoid taking a position where poverty and/or lack of alternatives is enough to invalidate consent because this would make it almost impossible for the poor to give valid consent to any transaction. He is also right to hold that the background conditions could be caused by the actions or omissions of another party who had a duty to prevent or alleviate poverty and provide better alternatives. We also agree that this is morally significant. The Indian State for one is probably just such a party.

There is, however, a serious problem. According to Wilkinson, there has to be an unfair distribution of benefits and invalid consent for a transaction to be exploitative. While we can certainly find many cases in which the background conditions are coercive, there are many more where they are caused by bad luck or misfortune, and this is where the implausible outcomes of applying Wilkinson's consent condition arise. Consider the following:

1. Bandini faces destitution if she does not accept the Allbrights' unfairly low pay for the surrogacy arrangement. She is capable of giving informed consent, and her circumstances are caused by the state's neglect of its duties towards her. She is exploited.
2. Bandini faces destitution if she does not accept the Allbrights' unfairly low pay for the surrogacy arrangement. She is capable of giving informed consent and her circumstances are caused by misfortune. She is not exploited.

Bandini's actual situation is identical in each scenario, and it seems odd to describe one as exploitation and the other not. The cause of her background conditions seems irrelevant to whether she is exploited or not (Malmqvist 2013). And in each case, the remedy is the same: if we change the Allbrights' offer to a fair one, neither scenario involves exploitation. The state continues its neglect of its duties to Bandini, which is a serious concern, but she is no longer being exploited. It appears that the unjust distribution of benefits and harms is the condition that matters and that invalid consent is a separate issue.

Fair Price

If we want to say that the Allbrights' offer to Bandini is unfair, then we have to be able to say what would be a fair price. Fair pay is one aspect of justice and, if we are concerned only with that, we might say that the fair price is what Bandini would get in a competitive market where she could charge according to the value of her services. If a couple is prepared to pay more than the Allbrights, then she would accept their offer. That could happen only if the market was genuinely competitive. We can compare the Allbrights' offer with this 'hypothetical market price' and, if it is lower, say that they are taking unfair advantage of her (Wertheimer 1996: 230). Of course, there are many ways to take advantage of people and to treat them unjustly. Paying a fair price would not solve those problems. But to determine a fair price for surrogacy arrangements is an important step forward, and we argue that it can be done.

Transactions are usually evaluated by assessing the contract and judging whether the terms and conditions are fair. If Bandini was working in a garment factory as sweated labour, it would be relatively easy to assess the contract. The value of her output and the pay she received could be directly compared in the same terms. Surrogacy is different. The Allbrights receive a baby and Bandini receives payment. The benefits are not the same kind of thing so they cannot be directly compared.

Vida Panitch's work on justice and exploitation is helpful in this regard. She argues that comparing the value of the surrogate's ability to provide benefits for her own family with the benefit that the intended parents receive goes some way towards assessing the fairness of the agreement. For example, if Bandini was able to send her own children to school as a result of the payment she received, that would be a benefit more similar to the Allbrights' benefit. However, it is not enough to look just at the contract between Bandini and the Allbrights. An important principle of justice is that there is equal pay for equal work. That means the pay and conditions for Bandini in India should be comparable to those of her counterparts in the US. If they are, then Bandini might not be exploited (Panitch 2013: 332). If the burden of pregnancy and childbirth is the same for surrogates in both countries, comparing the pay and conditions of a US surrogate and an Indian one provides a better way of judging whether the contract is exploitative. Panitch cautiously assumes that there is a reliable measure of purchasing power parity and concludes that Indian surrogates quite possibly are similarly remunerated. However, she thinks that the comparison of non-financial benefits is more robust and argues that the Indian arrangements are unjust because US surrogates enjoy the following benefits that Indian surrogates do not:

> The freedom to pursue other interests while under contract, health care, travel and dietary expenses, legal representation, a post-birth opt-out clause, and the potential for a rewarding relationship with the adoptive family. (Panitch 2013: 332–333)

It is also possible that pregnancy and childbirth are riskier for poor women in India than for women in the US so the injustice to them is even greater. If Panitch is right, then we can determine a fair price for surrogacy arrangements by looking across contracts. However, comparing contracts will only work if the better contract is not itself exploitative. It could be the case that US surrogates are exploited but less so than Indian surrogates. Our account of exploitation must be able to test that possibility as well.

Taking Advantage of Unfairness

The context in which a transaction takes place is important, as we have seen. However, there are also risks to focusing on the context instead of just on the transaction itself. If the principal fault is thought to lie elsewhere, it is easy to overlook the duties that individual exploiters have towards the exploited. Panitch correctly identifies the Indian State as the party that has the duty to rescue its people from poverty. She is also correct to say that the intended parents do not have a duty to rescue Indian women from poverty. The intended parents have no special responsibility towards Indian women because they have not caused the poverty. They have only the same general duty to alleviate poverty as the rest of the rich world. Many intended parents prefer to use Indian surrogates because it is less expensive to do so. That on its own is not wrongful. It is unfair that some countries are richer than others and there are many causes of that unfairness that have little to do with blameworthy actions. Taking advantage of unfairness is not wrong in itself. Low-income countries depend on high-income countries taking advantage of that unfairness because it is what makes their economies competitive and enables them to trade their way out of poverty. They depend on the disparity of value in labour costs. Once labour costs go up, they find it difficult to compete. All that is true. But it is not the end of the story. A fair price is intended to prevent the *unfair* taking advantage of unfairness (to use Wertheimer's phrasing). For example, if the intended parents paid only the cheapest price they could get away with, this would be taking unfair advantage. But the fair price in transnational surrogacy will still be lower than it is in richer countries. It follows that intended parents *do* have a duty towards the surrogate: to pay the fair price just as corporations have a duty to pay their employees the fair price. The predicament corporations often find themselves in is that it is not possible to pay the fair price and stay in business (Mayer 2007a). This is instructive for evaluating surrogacy arrangements.

Mutually Advantageous Exploitation

The category of mutually advantageous exploitation is necessary precisely because agreeing to an exploitative arrangement can be the better option for Bandini. Bandini may be better off being exploited if the alternative is no job at all. How we evaluate the actions of the exploiters in these cases depends on whether the exploitation is avoidable or not. Suppose the clinic that recruited Bandini wants to pay her a fair price. It would charge the Allbrights accordingly. But if other clinics could charge less by paying their surrogates badly, they would have a competitive advantage that could lead to Bandini's clinic going bankrupt. That would leave Bandini destitute or working for another clinic where she will be paid an unfairly low price. Such situations arise in countries with poor regulation or regulation that is not enforced. With those background conditions, the clinics have a choice between paying their surrogates unfairly and going out of business, leaving the women destitute because there are so few alternatives. That kind of exploitation is unavoidable (or structural) exploitation (Mayer 2007a: 605–606).

The situation is different if the exploitation is avoidable (known as discretionary exploitation). If paying Bandini the fair price would not put the clinic out of business, then the clinic and the Allbrights have a duty to pay it. If the background conditions in which the clinics operate are such that they would not go bankrupt if they paid their surrogates fairly, then they have no excuse for exploiting them and it is not permissible to do so. Given the difference it makes to the moral evaluation of exploitative practices, it is important to determine whether the exploitation is unavoidable (structural) and possibly permissible or avoidable (discretionary) and never acceptable.

To sum up:

1. Unfairly low pay in a transaction is enough for it to be exploitation.
2. A fair price can be determined.
3. Sometimes exploitation is mutually advantageous.
4. It is possible, and often reasonable, for the weaker party to consent to an exploitative transaction.
5. Sometimes exploitation is unavoidable and paying an unfair price is acceptable.
6. Avoidable exploitation is never permissible.

Permissible Exploitation

Although transnational surrogacy is often exploitative, in many cases it is also mutually advantageous. Banning it would, therefore, leave women worse off. Unless comparable alternative employment is available, mitigating exploitation through better regulation and improved legal protections is preferable to a ban. In what follows, we examine in detail the nature of the exploitation in transnational surrogacy and the responsibilities of the intended parents who use it. Mitigating exploitation involves all parties to the transactions, not just the clinics or the state.

While there is extensive (and justified) criticism of some intended parents, they are generally viewed positively. They see themselves and are seen by others as providing an opportunity for impoverished women to escape poverty, improve the life chances of their own children and avoid the much more hazardous low-paid occupations that are the only alternative to surrogacy. If that were the case, then the Allbrights would not be exploiting Bandini because a payment that alleviated her poverty would not constitute taking unfair advantage of her.

If Bandini were somewhat better off but not so well off as she would have been, then it is a case of mutually advantageous exploitation. Permitting the practice might then be justified because Bandini would be worse off if it was banned. We suspect that transnational surrogacy is usually mutually advantageous exploitation. It is unfair but not as bad as the alternatives for Bandini.

If she was left in her financially precarious state, no better off than she would have been with any of the alternatives, then it would be exploitation with no redeeming features and its permissibility would be seriously questioned (Kirby 2014; Wilkinson 2015).

Although intended parents believe that they transform the lives of these women, recent research suggests that the benefits to the women are not, on the whole, life-changing, that they receive far less remuneration than is reported, have far lower quality of clinical care than the agencies state and that they face additional costs as a result of undertaking surrogate pregnancies, such as child care, while they are living in the clinics' accommodation (Rudrappa and Collins 2015; Reddy and Patel 2015; White 2014). The fact that some women act as surrogates more than once suggests that poverty alleviation is less common than it is widely held to be (Karandikar et al. 2014). Why do the intended parents persist in their mistaken beliefs? Sharmila Rudrappa and Caitlyn Collins (2015) report that this is partly due to the careful management of information by the agencies and clinics who often prevent the intended parents from meeting the surrogate and leave them with only the carefully crafted profiles to study. Those who attempt to find out the truth for themselves are blocked from doing so and most of the couples in their sample did not even try.

It is important to bear in mind that the intended parents exploit the surrogates even if they sincerely, but mistakenly, believe that the terms of the transaction are fair. Exploitation need not be intentional (Wertheimer 1996: 209). The intended parents' may be less culpable in such cases. We argue, however, that the intended parents are not entitled to hold their beliefs and are not free of moral responsibility for the exploitation.

Fair Compensation

If Bandini is being exploited, who is morally responsible for it? Again, that depends on whether the exploitation is avoidable or not. It does seem that many of the conditions that Bandini and her sister surrogates endure are avoidable. Although Panitch is open to the possibility that the payment is fair, we think that the payment tends to be unfairly low. If increasing payment to surrogates would put the clinics out of business, then the exploitation would be unavoidable, though mutually advantageous. The intended parents could not be held wholly responsible for it. However, that does not mean that the unjust conditions in which they live are unavoidable.

It is very clear from the studies of Indian surrogates that the conditions they endure are often unjust. The hostels they have to live in are often dirty, the quality of the food poor and the staff ill-treat them (Saravanan 2013). Yet the cost of providing clean accommodation, nutritious food and decent treatment would not be that much greater than the current inadequate fare. It costs nothing to treat someone with courtesy rather than hostility. Allowing more visits from family, especially the surrogates' own children, would not be difficult to organize and if the women were being well cared for there would be no reason to prevent their families from seeing them. The current failings are indicative of a general contempt for women, particularly poverty stricken ones, in that society. But if the conditions were improved—to the level that the intended parents are led to believe exist already—the change would eliminate a significant amount of ill-treatment.

The clinics would not go out of business if they treated the women well. However, surrogacy providers would object that clinics that continued with unjust practices would have a small competitive advantage that might make a difference to the profitability of 'good' clinics. And, because of poor regulatory oversight, the 'bad' clinics would continue their practices with impunity. In other words, they would claim that *all* the exploitation is unavoidable. No one disputes the claim that the Indian State neglects its duty to regulate surrogacy clinics nor that endemic corruption makes it difficult to eliminate abuses, but the State is not the only powerful actor in the industry. We argue that the clients, people like the Allbrights, have enough power to influence the quality of the clinics significantly. Currently, they do not use it. To the extent that the exploitation is avoidable and within the power of intended parents to remove, we think they have a duty to do so.

When states fail in their duties to vulnerable citizens, everyone has a duty to help the destitute and desperate when they have the means and the opportunity to do so. For example, in natural disasters, if the state's response is inadequate, charities and individuals step in. We do not, as a general rule, let people die of starvation, cold or disease and say it is the state's responsibility and no one else's to provide emergency relief. People who are in a position to do something do it because the need is there. Emergencies are very visible and immediate. Chronic poverty is easier to overlook, especially when it is in distant countries. However, for people who use transnational surrogacy, the poverty of those providing the services is one of the dominant features of the arrangements and they are in a position to provide very direct and transformative assistance to those individuals if they choose to. So the Allbrights have a duty to Bandini and are much better situated than anyone else to act on it. If they do not alleviate her poverty as much as possible and ensure she is treated well, they have failed in their duty towards her.

Information about the actual conditions of Indian surrogates is readily available. Intended parents should also be aware of the way they are being managed by the clinics and prevented from seeing for themselves that the surrogates are properly cared for. Some common practices make the intended parents directly responsible for the ill-treatment of surrogates. Multiple embryo transfer, fetal reduction and unnecessary Caesarean sections are all harmful procedures, and they are all avoidable. Intended parents can say no to all of them. It raises their costs to do so and may be inconvenient but those are consequences they are morally obliged to accept.

In some cases, it will be difficult to determine whether the exploitation is avoidable or not but once it is clear, there is no doubt about what to do. However, we do not underestimate the difficulty of applying the remedies.

Unavoidable (structural) exploitation is harder to deal with. An outright ban on transnational surrogacy would leave Bandini worse off. If the exploitation is unavoidable, then attempts to improve her share of the benefits would put the clinic out of business and she would be worse off. That is what unavoidable exploitation means: there is no alternative that leaves Bandini better off. It appears that we would have to let the Allbrights continue exploiting Bandini. However, that does not make exploitation morally good. Nor does it mean that exploitation is the only wrong being done. The Allbrights may be the only ones directly responsible for the exploitation but other parties are complicit in the underlying injustice that makes the exploitation possible (Malmqvist 2013).

Being Complicit in Injustice

Transnational surrogacy in the developing world takes place against a background of widespread injustice to its most vulnerable citizens. To take advantage of those unjust conditions is to become complicit in the reproduction of injustice, a wrong that is distinct from exploitation (Malmqvist 2015: 7). It is not just the intended parents who are complicit. They may be the most directly involved parties because they keep the clinics in business, but others are part of the process that sends intended parents to the developing world in the first place.

To be complicit is to contribute causally and knowingly to the wrongdoing of others. If you know, or should have known, that your actions could assist others to do wrong, then you are complicit, whether or not you intended to contribute. And complicity does not require that the wrongdoing eventuates, just that it could do so (Malmqvist 2015: 8–9).

Complicit parties assist wrongful exploitation in two ways: by providing incentives to the exploiter to oppose structural reforms that would put her out of business and/or by legitimizing the injustice (Malmqvist 2015). We can see both of these in transnational surrogacy. For example, the eagerness of the intended parents to minimize the cost of surrogacy provides an incentive to clinics to oppose reform and regulation that would protect surrogates and raise costs significantly. Also troubling is the way the intended parents' story about surrogacy hides the truth even from themselves. They have a 'rescue' narrative in which they take women out of poverty and give them lives they never could have achieved for themselves. The clinics, as we have seen, make sure they have no reason to doubt this 'fact'. The Allbrights could quite genuinely believe that they gave Bandini opportunities she would not have had but they are unlikely to ask themselves why Bandini needed rescuing in the first place. Poverty as a serious social justice issue does not figure in the story. Individuals saving individuals is what it is all about.

In our view, the home countries of the intended parents are also guilty of complicity in the reproduction of injustice in transnational surrogacy. The intended parents who use transnational surrogacy do so, by and large, because their home countries make domestic surrogacy extremely difficult for them. Domestic surrogacy arrangements tend to be illegal, prohibitively expensive, inefficiently regulated, unacceptably risky, or some combination of these. And governments *should* know that people will not simply abandon their plans to form a family through surrogacy, even when transnational surrogacy is banned as well. The practice simply goes underground where it is likely to be even more exploitative and dangerous for all parties.

Given that governments have considerably more power to change unjust conditions than individuals do, we think that the intended parents are less to blame than their home countries' governments for the reproduction of injustice in the case of transnational surrogacy. If it is not possible for a particular country to provide adequate domestic surrogacy services, then the government has the option of regulating the use of transnational providers by its citizens and should do so.

Domestic Surrogacy

Although we have focussed on transnational surrogacy, our account applies to domestic surrogacy as well. We think that domestic surrogacy is usually preferable to transnational surrogacy, which tends to be poorly regulated. However, that does not mean it cannot be exploitative. Some people think that surrogacy is inherently exploitative, but this position is difficult to maintain if the surrogates' own views are taken seriously (Jadva et al. 2003, 2015). A more plausible concern is that domestic surrogacy tends to be only less exploitative than transnational surrogacy. One argument for the exploitative nature of domestic, commercial surrogacy is that the surrogate is usually from a lower socio-economic group than the intended parents, which puts her at a disadvantage. It need not do so, but that is a real risk in jurisdictions where surrogacy is solely governed by contract law and not subject to rigorous regulation. Recourse for either party when something goes wrong is to the courts and the surrogate is less able to afford that.

We think that altruistic surrogacy is also exploitative, especially when it is the only form of surrogacy permitted. It often takes unfair advantage of a woman's generosity to others and imposes costs on her that she should not have to bear. It cannot even be considered an example of mutually advantageous exploitation because the surrogate is not better off than she would have been had she not entered the arrangement. She is worse off: it is an additional pregnancy for her with all the attendant physical consequences. In gestational surrogacy, her body is put through risky and unpleasant procedures that she would not normally need in order to establish a pregnancy. Where someone is worse off than they would have been had they done nothing, the practice is extremely difficult to justify. However, we do not think that it should be banned, as there are cases where a surrogate genuinely prefers not to be paid. Respect for the autonomy of surrogates requires that the option be available but, for reasons we set out in Chap. 6, it should be rare. It should not be a test of a woman's motivation.

There is no reason to believe that domestic surrogacy in rich countries is unavoidably exploitative. However, there are opportunities for avoidable exploitation to occur. We suspect that these are common, and an important objective of the professional model is to remove them. If domestic surrogacy was more widely available and countries only permitted the use of accredited transnational clinics, the exploitation of surrogates would be greatly reduced.

Commodification

The other main objection levelled against surrogacy, commercial in particular, is that of commodification. There are four versions of the claim. Women are objectified and treated solely as means to an end (Saravanan 2010; Snow 2016; Tieu 2009); babies become commodities to be bought and sold (Baylis 2014; Fenton-Glynn 2016; Fronek and Crawshaw 2015; McLachlan and Swales 2009; Scott 2009); a woman's body parts and/or agency are being sold (Fenton-Glynn 2016; Fronek and Crawshaw 2015; Panitch 2015; Reddy and Patel 2015; Scott 2009); and finally, the special nature of the mother/child bond or motherhood itself is broken by commodifying women and babies (Snow 2016; Tieu 2009).

What Is Commodification?

A commodity has a monetary value and is fully interchangeable. For example, coffee is coffee and milk is milk. You might choose low-fat milk rather than full-fat milk but you will buy any bottle of that low-fat milk. To commodify persons is to treat them as having a monetary value and as being fully interchangeable.

According to Wilkinson (2003a: 27), commodification is a form of objectification. There are a number of ways to objectify a person. She can be treated as an instrument, have her autonomy denied, be treated as interchangeable with anyone else, have her bodily integrity breached, be treated as property or have her existence as a subject denied (Nussbaum 1995: 257; Wilkinson 2003a: 28). Persons should never be treated simply as a means to an end nor should they have their dignity denied. But, when someone is objectified, either or both of these things happen. Putting a price on someone is a denial of their dignity. They are being objectified and commodified (Wilkinson 2003a: 30). It is not wrong to treat people as means. What is wrong is to treat them merely as means, for example when their employer sees them only as instruments to be used without seeing them as people who have interests and desires of their own.

Surrogates as Commodities

How should we evaluate the claim that surrogacy involves commodification? There is enough evidence to show that some of the commodification claims are correct for surrogacy as it currently operates, especially in transnational surrogacy. Sheela Saravanan (2010) studied Indian surrogates and found that the women were expected to submit to all procedures without question, to accept the terms of the contract without negotiation, including a long list of rules regarding accommodation. A woman who objected to anything would be replaced. If attempts to establish a pregnancy for a couple failed, then another woman would be selected. There was no recognition of a surrogate's care for the baby she had carried and no concern over her welfare after relinquishment. While the feelings surrogates have for the intended baby are not maternal, there is a connection and most surrogates have an interest in how the baby gets on. Regrettably, one of the attractions of transnational surrogacy for intended parents is that the surrogate can be cut out of the picture as soon as they take the baby from her. These are all ways of objectifying the surrogate and treating her as a commodity, and pose a clear risk where the practice is poorly regulated. However, they are not inevitable in surrogacy and could be mitigated. The remedy is to regulate it better, with a clear understanding of the necessary ethical foundations to do so. That is what we hope to provide in this book.

Reproductive Organs as Commodities

Some critics of surrogacy worry about the commodification of women's reproductive organs, a form of body parts objectification, but this is difficult to support except in those cases where there is no valid consent to their use. The fact that people can validly consent to all the procedures that surrogacy involves suggests that more effort should be put into ensuring that surrogates are indeed giving valid consent. In the case of transnational surrogacy, there are significant concerns about consent but we should focus on the way the clinics operate rather than on the women themselves. They may be illiterate and impoverished but, clearly, researchers regard them as able to give valid consent. If clinics used the same methods to gain consent, such as reading all the information to the women, including the terms of the contract, in their own language, giving them a copy of the contract, explaining the procedures in terms that they understand and ensuring that they are aware of the risks, then consent could be valid. Consent is not a substitute for regulation, however. Practices that are dangerous should be banned everywhere. We discuss these issues in Chap. 6.

Babies as Commodities

The other version of the commodification claim, namely that babies become commodities, is very difficult to substantiate. People assume that, because money changes hands, a baby is being bought and sold. However, neither babies nor parental rights can be sold (McLachlan and Swales 2009). The legal parentage of a child is a matter for the courts to determine. Arrangements that are found to involve payment for a child will be void and probably subject to criminal investigation. Both national and international laws come into play when babies are commodified. However, it could be argued that when a court upholds a commercial surrogacy arrangement by transferring parental rights, the baby has indeed changed hands for money because, without the money, there would have been no baby.

Let us assume that the arrangement would not have been possible without payment to the surrogate. In that sense, it is true that a baby exists as the result of a financial transaction. But whose baby it is, is not determined by that transaction. Even in places where most of a contract is enforceable, the transfer of parental rights is a clause that will not be. That is the point at which the exchange of money could count against the arrangement being upheld. Consider an altruistic arrangement and a commercial one where the only difference is the payment. The people are the same and the baby is the same. It happens in a state that permits both altruistic and commercial surrogacy. When the intended parents apply for legal parentage, the court will use exactly the same criteria to determine who the baby's parents should be. The money will either make no difference or count against it.

What if a surrogate repays the money so that she can keep the baby? Has she refunded its purchase price? No. In any jurisdiction where the surrogate is the legal mother, the only setting where transfers are required, she has the right to change her mind irrespective of what happens over the money. Nor does it guarantee that she will keep custody of the baby. If the court or welfare authorities have sufficient concerns over her parenting ability, they can remove the baby from her care. They can do this to any parent. The courts have the power to terminate anyone's parental rights and place a child for adoption. Children cannot be owned. The payments intended parents make to surrogates cannot give effect to parental rights.

Surrogates and intended parents are often ignorant of the legal status of the child and what they themselves can and cannot dictate. The professional model eliminates the transfer of parental rights so there can be no suggestion of a baby changing hands for money and no doubt for the people involved about where their rights and responsibilities lie with respect to the child.

Conclusion

The most serious objections to surrogacy are that it is inherently exploitative and commodifies women and babies. Although surrogacy can be exploitative, we argued that it is not necessarily so. Surrogates are exploited when they are unfairly paid, as frequently happens in commercial surrogacy, or not paid at all, as in altruistic surrogacy. Transnational surrogacy is often exploitative. However, when the background conditions are such that exploitation is unavoidable, it can still be advantageous for a woman to act as a surrogate because the alternatives would leave her worse off. Such exploitation is sometimes permissible. However, we argued that avoidable exploitation is never acceptable and that surrogacy should be reformed to minimize it. The conditions transnational surrogates endure could easily be improved.

Commodification occurs when women are regarded as interchangeable and having a monetary value. It is a form of objectification. Surrogates are commodified if they are treated as mere means, have their autonomy denied or their bodily integrity breached. We argued that transnational surrogacy frequently does objectify women but that such commodification is not inevitable. Practices can and should be modified to eliminate it. Claims that commercial surrogacy necessarily commodifies babies by selling them cannot be substantiated because parental rights are determined solely by the legal system, not through the exchange of money. In fact, the attempted purchase of parental rights would normally result in being denied them, and possibly criminal charges as well.

At the time of writing, India has banned foreigners from using surrogacy clinics there, unless the couple is of Indian origin, but it has not implemented any regulatory policies to protect the surrogates' rights. The problem of exploitation remains, but the class of exploiters is smaller. Harm reduction or minimization is a valuable aim to have but good regulation could do a great deal more to end exploitation and commodification. They are the two biggest risks to women who act as surrogates but, as we have shown, not quite in the way people assume. However, they are not the only risks surrogates face. The following chapter explores the underlying nature of surrogacy relationships themselves, which have characteristics that leave surrogates vulnerable to a form of harm that neither altruistic nor commercial models of surrogacy acknowledge.

References

Baylis, F. (2014). Transnational commercial contract pregnancy in India. In F. Baylis & C. McLeod (Eds.), *Family-making: Contemporary ethical challenges* (pp. 265–286). Oxford: Oxford University Press.

Fenton-Glynn, C. (2016). Outsourcing ethical dilemmas: Regulating international surrogacy arrangements. *Medical Law Review, 24*(1), 59–75.

Fronek, P., & Crawshaw, M. (2015). The 'new family' as an emerging norm: A commentary on the position of social work in assisted reproduction. *British Journal of Social Work, 45*(2), 737–746.

Jadva, V., Imrie, S., & Golombok, S. (2015). Surrogate mothers 10 years on: A longitudinal study of psychological well-being and relationships with the parents and child. *Human Reproduction, 30*(2), 373–379.

Jadva, V., Murray, C., Lycett, E., & Golombok, S. (2003). Surrogacy: The experiences of surrogate mothers. *Human Reproduction, 18*(10), 2196–2204.

Karandikar, S., Gezinski, L. B., Carter, J. R., & Kaloga, M. (2014). Economic necessity or noble cause? A qualitative study exploring motivations for gestational surrogacy in Gujarat, India. *Affilia, 29*(2), 224–236.

Kirby, J. (2014). Transnational gestational surrogacy: Does it have to be exploitative? *American Journal of Bioethics, 14*(5), 24–32.

Malmqvist, E. (2013). Taking advantage of injustice. *Social Theory & Practice, 39*(4), 557–580.

Malmqvist, E. (2015). Better to exploit than to neglect? International clinical research and the non-worseness claim. *Journal of Applied Philosophy.* DOI: 10.1111/japp.12153.

Mayer, R. (2007a). Sweatshops, exploitation, and moral responsibility. *Journal of Social Philosophy, 38*(4), 605–619.

Mayer, R. (2007b). What's wrong with exploitation? *Journal of Applied Philosophy, 24*(2), 137–150.

McLachlan, H. V., & Swales, J. K. (2009). Commercial surrogate motherhood and the alleged commodification of children: A defense of legally enforceable contracts. *Law and Contemporary Problems, 72*(3), 91–107.

Nussbaum, M. C. (1995). Objectification. *Philosophy & Public Affairs, 24*(4), 249–291.

Panitch, V. (2013). Global surrogacy: Exploitation to empowerment. *Journal of Global Ethics, 9*(3), 329–343.

Panitch, V. (2015). Commodification and exploitation in reproductive markets: Introduction to the symposium on reproductive markets. *Journal of Applied Philosophy, 33*(2), 117–124.

Reddy, S., & Patel, T. (2015). "There are many eggs in my body": Medical markets and commodified bodies in India. *Global Bioethics, 26*(3–4), 218–231.

Rudrappa, S., & Collins, C. (2015). Altruistic agencies and compassionate consumers: Moral framing of transnational surrogacy. *Gender & Society, 29*(6), 937–959.

Saravanan, S. (2010). Transnational surrogacy and objectification of gestational mothers. *Economic and Political Weekly, 45*(16), 26–29.

Saravanan, S. (2013). An ethnomethodological approach to examine exploitation in the context of capacity, trust and experience of commercial surrogacy in India. *Philosophy, Ethics, and Humanities Medicine, 8*(10), 1–12.

Scott, E. S. (2009). Surrogacy and the politics of commodification. *Law and Contemporary Problems, 72*(3), 109–146.

Snow, D. (2016). Criminalising commercial surrogacy in Canada and Australia: The political construction of 'national consensus'. *Australian Journal of Political Science, 51*(1), 1–16.

Tieu, M. M. (2009). Altruistic surrogacy: The necessary objectification of surrogate mothers. *Journal of Medical Ethics, 35*(3), 171–175.

Wertheimer, A. (1996). *Exploitation.* Princeton, NJ: Princeton University Press.

White, G. (2014). Gestational surrogates in rural India: A lot to offer and even more to lose. *American Journal of Bioethics, 14*(5), 40–42.

Wilkinson, S. (2003a). *Bodies for sale: Ethics and exploitation in the human body trade.* London: Routledge.

Wilkinson, S. (2003b). The exploitation argument against commercial surrogacy. *Bioethics, 17*(2), 169–187.

Wilkinson, S. (2015). Exploitation in international paid surrogacy arrangements. *Journal of Applied Philosophy, 33*(2), 125–145.

3

Altruism and Generosity

Introduction

Is surrogacy best viewed as a closed-ended business transaction or an open-ended personal relationship? Proponents of the commercial model would answer the former and proponents of the altruistic model the latter. Based on these assumptions about the nature of the relationship they advocate reform of current models. We take a different view. We argue that fundamentally all surrogacy relationships, whether paid or unpaid, domestic or transnational, are driven by the same underlying social mechanism. They are all gift exchanges. The gift exchange mechanism underpins an extensive range of interactions between people, not just gift-giving. It is important to understand that it operates without being consciously or intentionally applied. Once surrogacy is analysed in terms of gift exchange it is clear why the two models fail to solve the problems that arise. It also becomes possible to see how surrogacy arrangements could be structured to improve the experience for surrogates and intended parents. Gift exchanges generate intuitive expectations and obligations. When relationships are forced into a framework that runs counter to these expectations the result is deep ambiguity

© The Author(s) 2017
R. Walker and L. van Zyl, *Towards a Professional Model of Surrogate Motherhood*,
DOI 10.1057/978-1-137-58658-2_3

about the nature of the relationship, which can lead to the two parties to one relationship having different answers to the questions posed above. The results can be disastrous. To show how, we begin with the concept of gift and then move to gift exchange itself.

Gifts

In both altruistic and commercial arrangements, the dominant motif in describing the relationship between intended parents and surrogates is that of a 'gift'. It shares this with other forms of donation, including organs and gametes. Surrogacy has most in common with living organ donation, primarily of kidneys, although egg donors also undergo unpleasant procedures that carry risk of serious harm. In the organ donor literature, especially in the publicity designed to increase rates of donation, the idea of gift, particularly 'gift of life' is central. In one sense, organ donation is the gift of life, or the chance for continued life, as recipients would die without the transplant. Surrogates are giving life by gestating a baby that would not otherwise exist. On the surface, then, the description of their actions as a gift of life is unproblematic. However, it is not that simple. Gift relationships are a crucial, universal dimension of social interaction but they are far from straightforward. So, while intended parents and surrogates use the concept of 'gift' to describe their relationship, it would be naïve to assume that their relationship is an uncomplicated one.

Gift Exchange

To speak of a gift relationship is to suggest that a meaningful connection between two parties has been established through the giving and receiving of something significant. Organs are significant, but even something as apparently superficial as corporate gift-giving at Christmas can be significant because of what it symbolizes about business relationships (Lemmergaard and Muhr 2011). These examples look very different but they are explained by the same social mechanism: gift exchange.

Gift exchanges are extensively documented in anthropology and sociology. They have also been observed in other social species and evolutionary explanations of their survival value are well established. Aafke Komter, a well-known sociologist, argues that gift exchanges are based on reciprocity and that their function is to establish and stabilize social bonds within a wide range of human activity (Komter 2007). Although we tend to think of gifts and reciprocating as morally good, this is not always the case. Gifts can be used to 'manipulate, flatter, bribe, deceive, humiliate, dominate, offend, hurt and even kill' (Komter 2007: 94). Unsurprisingly, people are intensely sensitive to gift relationships and their status within them. Komter (2007: 98) adopts Fiske's four types of human gift relationship, namely 'community sharing', 'authority ranking', 'equality matching' and 'market pricing'. Each type has a different basis and associated motivations. The two that are particularly relevant to surrogacy are 'community sharing' and 'market pricing'.

Community Sharing and Market Pricing Relationships

Community sharing relationships are based on 'feelings of connectedness' or 'identification with other people'. Gifts are given because of perceived need and often include 'food, care, or services.' By contrast, market pricing relationships, such as corporate gift-giving, are transactional, instrumental, and based on benefits outweighing costs. The motives behind community sharing and market pricing relationships differ considerably. Community sharing involves motives that are directed towards the good of others, such as 'friendship, love, gratitude, respect, loyalty or solidarity.' (Komter 2007: 99). However, in market pricing the motivation is 'implicit or explicit self-interest.' (Komter 2007: 100). Gift relationships do not come with labels so it is possible to be mistaken both about the nature of the relationship and one's status within it.

While surrogates and intended parents tend to describe their relationship in terms of a gift, very often there is a mismatch between the two parties' understanding of the type of gift relationship they are in, which is further complicated by the changes that occur over the course of the pregnancy. Surrogates tend to treat the relationship as a 'community sharing' one, while the intended parents treat it as a 'market pricing' one, with the result that their perceptions, motivations and expectations can be very different. Occasionally this mismatch occurs unintentionally, but, as we will see, it is often encouraged by the intended parents. Uncertainty about the nature of the relationship causes many of the difficulties experienced in surrogacy.

There is considerable evidence that surrogates are responding to a need in other people with whom they identify. They feel sympathy for couples who cannot have children and want to help. Their motivations are indeed strongly focussed on the needs of others and they frequently speak in terms of love and friendship. Gestational care is a form of care and service and so is an example of the typical gift in community sharing relationships. The motivations reported in the literature are similar across widely divergent populations and forms of surrogacy arrangement. In the state-regulated commercial system in Israel, Elly Teman (2010) found that surrogates used metaphors, such as marriage, to describe the intimate bond they had formed with the intended mother. They spoke of love and care for her, helping her to become the mother of the baby they were carrying for her. Amrita Pande's (2014) participants in an Indian surrogacy clinic often referred to their intended mother as their sister and believed that was how the intended mother saw them as well. Zsuzsa Berend (2012) reports that commercial surrogates in the US described the initial relationship in terms of falling in love, being a perfect match, and finding the couple that was destined for them. In turn, intended parents seem to want their surrogates to be motivated by a desire to help them rather than by financial considerations. They describe surrogates who appear to be doing it for altruistic reasons in very approving terms even if they themselves see the relationship rather differently (Murphy 2015). There may be no intention to manipulate or deceive the surrogates (although sometimes there is) but their behaviour towards the surrogate during the pregnancy can indicate to her that they feel the same way about her as she does about them. When it changes after the baby is handed over, whether abruptly or gradually, it can be devastating for the surrogate. But it should not be surprising that it happens if the intended parents believe the relationship to be one of market pricing.

There is nothing inherently wrong with market pricing relationships where both parties understand that that is what it is and where it is appropriate for the type of exchange. In a good quality market pricing relationship, both parties would feel that the benefits exceeded the costs and that it served their purposes. These relationships establish and stabilize the business interactions on which societies depend. And while the relationship is instrumental, that does not imply that the other party herself is regarded as an instrument or object. However, where there is a mismatch or the type of exchange involved is not best treated as a market pricing relationship, difficulties arise. For the intended parents, it may seem obvious that the surrogacy arrangement is a transaction that comes to an end. If they have paid the fees and met all the transactional requirements, the temporary relationship with the surrogate is over and they move to the next stage of their lives. They were entitled to act in their own interests, may have assumed that that was what the surrogate was doing as well and that further contact was not necessary. That is the kindest interpretation of their behaviour. There is plenty of evidence, however, that the intended parents frequently do encourage the surrogate to believe that the relationship is more personal and that it will continue. The termination of the relationship can be brutal. Berend (2012: 927) reports the experience of a surrogate, Tessa:

> Tessa told them they were unappreciative of the gift she had given them, to which her [Intended Father] responded that he had "no reason to be appreciative." After all, Tessa "did not do anything" for them that "she wasn't paid to do." This was a business transaction, he told her; they paid in full and had no reason to be grateful.

The reason the intended father had the power to exploit the ambiguity of the relationship with Tessa was because the nature of the gift relationship is not made explicit in current models of surrogacy. However, describing the relationship clearly is not enough. We also need to consider what sort of relationship it should be. Should it be a community sharing one or a market pricing one? To return to the question we posed at the beginning of the chapter, is surrogacy best viewed as a closed-ended business transaction or an open-ended personal relationship? If the intended parents want their surrogates to be motivated by a desire to help them, as in a community sharing relationship, then it seems only right that they act as the other party should in a community sharing relationship. This is where the moral content of gift exchange is relevant.

Moral Obligations in Gift Exchanges

Gift exchange and the principle of reciprocity are closely tied to moral obligations. Following Marcel Mauss, Komter identifies three obligations arising from gift exchange: 'the obligation to give, the obligation to receive and the obligation to reciprocate.' (Komter 2007: 103). Failure to meet any one of these jeopardizes the social relationships on which survival depends. The principle of reciprocity is indispensable. Komter adds four more elements that explain why reciprocity is effective: 'the survival value of gift-giving; the recognition of the other implied in reciprocity; the morally binding character of reciprocity; and the fact that reciprocity combines generosity with self-interest.' (2007: 101) [original numbering omitted].

These features apply even in business to business relationships. In their study of corporate Christmas gift-giving between Danish businesses, Jeanette Lemmergaard and Sara Muhr (2011: 770–772) describe such gift-giving as an 'economy of regard' reporting that businesses that did not receive expected gifts felt neglect. The state of the business relationship was signalled by whether a gift was given at all rather than by what was given. There are emotional factors at play in all interactions and the authors argue that '[m]ost personal interactions are driven by the desire for attention and regard' (Lemmergaard and Muhr 2011: 774). So even if surrogacy were a market pricing relationship, there would still be emotional factors to consider.

Surrogacy and Community Sharing

We think that surrogacy is closest to being a community sharing relationship. The type of relationship determines what the appropriate forms of reciprocation will be. Consider first the 'recognition of the other implied in reciprocity.' Given what the surrogate has actually done, a cheque does not fully recognize her in a meaningful way. She should certainly be paid but she has given of herself bodily and emotionally to both the intended baby and to the intended parents who need her to undergo arduous and risky procedures. Surrogates do talk about a bond that they have with the child they carry (Pande 2014). They see the blood tie they have through gestation as giving both nourishment and identity to the baby (Pande 2009: 383). Intended parents who keep in touch with updates and photographs as the child grows up are giving the surrogate the right sort of recognition. They do not have to go on giving material gifts but they should include the surrogate in the child's story. To do so is to acknowledge the 'morally binding character of reciprocity'. They are carrying out their obligation to reciprocate. It is not just that the child has a right to know its origins but that the surrogate has the right to be visible, and not to be erased as so many of them are. Given her generosity, the intended parents should be generous in return. We discuss the vital role of generosity in reciprocation below. First, however, we need to address another form of ambiguity with regard to the status of the parties in the relationship.

Kinship and Social Connectedness

Kinship and social connectedness play an important role in determining the motives attached to gift-giving. There is a clear hierarchy. Close kin and connections receive 'disinterested gifts where no (immediate) returns are expected.' At the next level there is 'more or less equivalent reciprocity attended by clear expectations of returns.' Community sharing relationships belong in the first two levels depending on closeness of connection. The most distant connections use barter, which is 'mainly motivated by expected gains.' (Komter 2010: 453). Barter describes a market relationship between people who have no other relationship on which to base trust and generosity. Surrogacy arrangements between people who are not related and do not know each other are unexpectedly difficult because of 'kin work' (Pande 2009) within them. Gift exchanges between closely related people do not require immediate reciprocation because the relationship is a continuing one in which people can expect help when they need it even if this occurs a long time after the gift. The amount of uncertainty around the gift relationship tends to be less.

Something confusing happens in surrogacy. As we saw above, surrogates often form family-like bonds with the intended mother, in particular, even when they hardly see each other, which was the case for Pande's participants. For those who are in close contact with each other, as with Teman's surrogates, it is even more intimate. The levels of contact depend on many variables but what appears to happen is the development of 'fictive kinship' through the active work of the surrogate and the recognition of that work by the intended mother (Pande 2009, 2014). That changes the expectations of the surrogates because kinship usually means that the relationships are more permanent. The closer the kin, such as a sister, the more shared the life. But where there is no prior relationship between the intended parents and the surrogate to help guide what each should give, receive and reciprocate, fictive kinship can be dangerous for the surrogate.

Relational Devaluation

When disappointment occurs, the image of the gift is used as a means of social control over surrogates to shape what it is acceptable to object to and what it is not. Berend (2012) observed the way surrogates in an online support group coped with disappointment up to and including experiences, such as Tessa's quoted above. The first stage was to give the intended parents the benefit of the doubt for as long as possible and make allowances for them because it is so difficult with a new baby and they do not have time to keep in touch. However, in the face of undeniable evidence that they had been cutoff or could expect only the barest minimum of contact, they were not allowed by the rest of the group to 'whine' and had, instead, to focus on the wonderful gift that they had given. Terms such as being the intended parents' 'angel', in use while the relationship was still good, were retained. They gave and did not expect anything in return and that was the noblest gift of all. Berend (2014) argues that the context in which surrogates report satisfaction with what they have done has to be understood as at least partly shaped by whether it is permissible to express dissatisfaction and by how the social context operates to determine what counts as being satisfied and what level of contact counts as enough.

An alternative approach would take seriously the surrogates' expressions of sadness and loss. Because the literature is dominated by the assumption that what a surrogate ought to feel sad about is the loss of her baby, it overlooks the things that surrogates actually feel sad about, which are to do with the intended parents. When the problem is properly identified, it is possible to see what should be done about it. We think that the hurt that surrogates express is best understood as a response to relational devaluation. That is, they thought that they were highly valued by the intended parents and that the relationship was important to the intended parents. When they received signals that showed either that the relationship had never been what they thought it was or that they were much less valued than they thought they were, they responded with hurt feelings, sadness and loss. These were the dominant feelings although there was often anger as well. Edward Lemay et al. (2012) studied the functions of hurt feelings as a result of relational devaluation and found that they imply that 'the victim is vulnerable to psychological pain at the hands of the perpetrator, and this vulnerability likely comes about because the victim desires or needs a relationship with the perpetrator.' (Lemay et al. 2012: 983). The desire 'creates dependence and vulnerability', which leads to constructive actions by the victim to repair the relationship. This is in contrast to anger, which leads to aggressive and destructive acts. However, for the surrogates, once the intended parents have what they want—the baby— there is nothing the surrogate can do to re-establish a relationship that only she desires and needs. Relational devaluation is a significant risk for surrogates.

The ambiguity at the heart of the relationship allows such relational disasters to occur and makes surrogacy riskier than it needs to be. Unfortunately neither the altruistic nor the commercial model of surrogacy is capable of removing the ambiguity over the type of relationship surrogacy is. Indeed, some aspects of each model make it worse. The altruistic model makes unrealistic psychological demands on the surrogate and the commercial model reduces the relationship to a market pricing one without regard for the actual nature of the interactions. The situation is compounded by the 'gift of life' discourse that surrogacy shares with organ donation. In organ donation, it leads to difficulties for both donors and recipients that are very similar to the ones encountered in surrogacy.

Gift of Life

Organ donation and surrogacy literature predominantly use the 'gift of life' metaphor to describe what donors and surrogates give to their recipients. However, social scientists have raised concerns about its suitability for nearly two decades because of the dangers and pitfalls associated with gift-giving (Siminoff and Chillag 1999; Shaw and Webb 2015). Rhonda Shaw argues that by linking 'gift of life' to altruism and claiming for it the status of pure gift without the possibility of reciprocation, users of the discourse inflict real costs on both donors and recipients. For donors, gift of life discourse does not acknowledge the sacrifice that they make (Shaw 2010: 612). Deceased organ donation occurs in the context of trauma and tragedy, with the physical requirement to operate further on the person's body adding to the suffering of the family. The family makes a significant sacrifice rather than merely giving a gift. For this reason some physicians in Shaw's sample were very uncomfortable with gift terminology.

Living donors, who are most analogous to surrogates, are also making a sacrifice, usually for a family member. They may be doing so under pressure that might include violence (Scheper-Hughes 2007). Although violence might be very rare, there is reason to agree with Nancy Scheper-Hughes' argument that living donors are almost invisible and that the sacrifices demanded of them are inadequately acknowledged. The ethnographic studies in Egypt and Mexico conducted by Megan Crowley-Matoka and Sherine Hamdy (2016) support her concerns. They also document the gendered nature of living organ donation, especially where mothers' donation is seen as a natural and 'expected extension of maternal duties' (Crowley-Matoka and Hamdy 2016: 34). Gendering is not inevitable but women tend to donate more than men do. And because they are women, they often receive very little acknowledgement of their sacrifice and generosity.

The Tyranny of the Gift

Idealization of organ donation as a purely altruistic gift of life can be used as a form of social control over what donors may say about it and what they must deny. Negative emotions arising from the experience of sacrifice and suffering are unacceptable (Shaw 2012). This not only affects the donors and their families but also the recipients, because being the receiver of a gift has a dark side well enough established to have its own term: the 'tyranny of the gift'. It applies when the recipient is put in a position where they will never be able to meet the obligation to reciprocate and the gift becomes a source of indebtedness to the giver that cannot be discharged. In organ donation this happens because the gift has 'no physical or symbolic equivalent.' (Siminoff and Chillag 1999: 36). What can the recipient possibly give back to the donor (or donor's family) in exchange? They are encouraged by staff to show gratitude by looking after the gift through compliance with a burdensome and difficult regimen that will continue for the rest of their lives. This is a form of social control that creates its own burdens.

In spite of the attempts to force the gift of life into a model of one way giving and receiving, the people involved do not see it that way. They intuitively understand it in gift relationship terms (Shaw 2012). We think they are right to do so and agree with Shaw that some provision for expressing gratitude and reciprocation needs to be built into the current donation system. If the medical and nursing staff involved as well as the donors and recipients understood the nature of gift relationships, they would be able to acknowledge and accommodate the 'doubled nature' of the gift. Burdens could be lifted from the donors and recipients if there was some recognized way for recipients to express their gratitude to the donor and also to be open with staff and family about how hard their lives remain as a result of the treatment regimen.

Something analogous needs to happen in surrogacy. However, the question that arises first is why 'gift of life' and pure altruism are so highly valued when they are so clearly at odds with the social mechanisms at work. The concept of altruism has played an integral role in the development of policy regarding all forms of donation and surrogacy.

Altruism

Given that altruism is widely considered to be the ideal in surrogacy, organ, tissue, blood and gamete donation, defining it should be easy. It is not. Beyond taking altruistic to mean 'unpaid' and 'for the benefit of others,' the literature does not agree on much. For example, some commentators think altruism is about motivation (Bishop and Rees 2007; Dufner 2015; Pennings 2015), others think it describes acts (Pettersen 2012; Saunders 2012; Steinberg 2010). The degree of selflessness required varies. Some transplant specialists regard feeling good about donating as a reward that undermines the altruistic nature of the act (Fortin et al. 2010). At the other end of the spectrum, associations of altruism with 'gift' leave open the conceptual possibility of reciprocation as part of a gift exchange relationship (Shaw and Bell 2015; Komter 2010). For the most part, however, rewards or reciprocation are taken to be incompatible with altruism (Dufner 2015; Pennings 2015; Steinberg 2010).

Because motivation is so difficult to measure or discern, it appears that non-payment has become a proxy for altruism in donation and surrogacy policy. If someone is prepared to donate organs or carry a baby without compensation then it seems safe to regard them as motivated by altruism. Even if the focus is on the act itself, it appears more obviously altruistic if the person gets no material reward for doing it. And yet, in paid caring professions such as medicine and nursing, practitioners have been expected to provide altruistic care, a demand now more widely seen as unrealistic and damaging (Pettersen 2012; Steinberg 2010). In these cases, the marker for altruism is complete sacrifice of one's own needs in order to care for the patient.

Altruistic Care

Tove Pettersen (2012: 368) identifies four features of altruistic care. Such care is '(1) a selfless act, (2) provided unconditionally and (3) spontaneously (4) to particular human beings in need of care (5) for the sake of that person's best interests.' These characteristics apply to donation and surrogacy as well.

Embedded in the concept of altruism is an assumption that morality requires concern for others rather than self and that the more one's actions are directed towards others' benefit rather than one's own the better they are. So the unpaid surrogate attains a higher moral standard than a commercial surrogate, an altruistic organ donor is far more praiseworthy than a compensated one, and a burnt out doctor or nurse has done something heroic in putting her patients' interests ahead of her own at all times.

Fear also plays a part in keeping altruism as the ideal: fear of commodification in the case of surrogacy and organ donation and fear of unleashing callous health professionals on vulnerable patient populations in the case of medical staff, nurses in particular.

Altruism tends to be highly gendered. All surrogates are women, most living organ donors are women and nursing is still a predominantly female profession. Women who put forward claims for consideration of their own interests are viewed with suspicion and disapproval. They are expected to be more self-sacrificing than men and to be more caring towards others. But Pettersen (2012: 369) is clearly right when she draws attention to the fact that most moral theories require the person's own interests to be counted when she is determining the right course of action. This means that other people have an obligation to consider them when they are setting policy and defining professional standards. It is not acceptable to require self-sacrifice and impose heavy costs on people when they are doing something of value for others. Members of the caring professions have legitimate needs of their own that they are entitled to have respected in concrete ways. Similarly, organ donors and surrogates are entitled to have their needs met. This would include receiving the necessary health care during and after donating or giving birth. Reimbursement of expenses they incur should be automatic.

If, however, the needs of donors are acknowledged and met, the degree of altruism appears to have been reduced, which leads David Steinberg to define different grades of altruism. Purely altruistic actions are 'intentional and voluntary actions that aim to enhance the welfare of another person in the absence of any quid pro quo external rewards.' (Steinberg 2010: 249). An action can still be predominantly altruistic if the reward is 'of a relatively trivial nature' but if altruism is 'sufficiently compromised' it counts as 'a commercial transaction.' His example is related to surrogacy. 'Twenty thousand dollars given to a gestational carrier is a commercial transaction.' (Steinberg 2010: 251).

Although Steinberg thinks that altruistic actions should not be assumed to be moral, he does appear to regard them as better than commercial ones. This is an unconscious bias shared by others. In medical parlance 'compromised' has a technical meaning and does not mean 'morally sullied', but when a patient's immune system, for example, is compromised it is a negative state rather than a positive one. External rewards that compromise altruism come across as suspect if not tainted. Even though Steinberg does a good job explaining what altruism looks like in practice and is aware of the risks associated with expecting altruism, especially for women, he still falls victim to the general tendency to see altruism, the purer the better, as morally superior to compensated action. Whether the focus is on action or motivation, then, the concept of altruism is understood in terms of moral value. The more selfless it is, the closer it is to the ideal of pure altruism and the more self-interest creeps in, the further away from the ideal it is. It seems, then, that even if we cannot quite work out what altruism is, we know that it is a good thing.

However, altruism is a term that needs to be used carefully. Sometimes it is used to refer to a moral ideal. The altruist does things to benefit others while his opposite, the egoist, does things for his own benefit. They might both do the right thing but they will do it for different reasons. When used in this sense, altruism is an ideal to strive for. Giving the 'gift of life' is an example of referring to altruism as an ideal.

Descriptive Altruism

However, altruism has another meaning that has nothing to do with morality. It comes from biology where the concept of reciprocal altruism explains the assistance animals (including humans) give to each other. They will help even at a cost to themselves, especially if it is for their close kin, and they will get help in return. Helping close genetic relatives improves the chances of their shared genes surviving to reproduce. That is not to say that it is done consciously or intentionally. Altruism is an underlying mechanism.

It is important not to conflate this mechanistic sense of altruism with the moral sense. Morals tell us what should happen, what people should do. A mechanism explains how a phenomenon works. It is neutral as to whether it is good or bad. It describes all of its characteristics, including both benefits and costs, risks and rewards. There is a risk of conflating the moral and mechanistic senses of altruism because gift relationships belong in the category of altruism as a mechanism even though they seem to be about ideals that people hold to deliberately. When we refer to mechanisms to explain gift exchange we describe how gift exchanges actually function and not how they should function. Reciprocal altruism and the gift exchange mechanism are not ideals. Gift exchanges have a 'dark side'. Cheating is a significant risk. We have discussed the doubled nature of the gift above, showing it can be both gift and burden. Anthropology and sociology tell us how gift relationships work and what the risks and benefits are to people who enter into them. When we impose altruism as an ideal on people, whether donors, surrogates or caring professionals, we fail to acknowledge the dark side of these relationships with their risks and costs. We demand the impossible of individuals: they are to give without receiving. Moreover, they are to give unstintingly but not protect themselves from the costs of doing so.

The Costs of the Altruistic Ideal

There are real costs to altruism. Some of these are obvious. Jeremy Shearmur (2015) raises the concern that 'the more burdensome donation is, the less it would seem reasonable to ask people to donate for strangers.' (Shearmur 2015: 128). He also makes the point about women, in particular, being coerced by family into donating. Altruistic donation prevents people from doing something against their better judgement because of a financial incentive. However, that is only one way in which the voluntariness of their donation could be affected. There are others, coercion being one, which altruism cannot prevent. Altruism can also make some things worse. Unpaid donation imposes financial costs on the donor in addition to those directly associated with donating. The altruistic model of donation, where donors are required to demonstrate that they have the right motivation, prevents them from raising the matter of financial reimbursement for lost wages and expenses incurred while they recover (Shaw and Bell 2015).

The requirement that donation be altruistic also imposes costs on society in the form of shortages of donors. Those willing to do it might not be able to afford to. Here, it would seem that the similarities between live organ donation and surrogacy break down. No one dies if they cannot have a family, and no one ends up in poverty because they cannot have children. Proponents of adoption would prefer couples to give homes to children who already exist rather than creating more. However, it is not that clear cut. What actually happens with a shortage of surrogates is that people take risks to form a family in spite of the legal and ethical ramifications of doing so. Private arrangements and use of transnational surrogacy, regardless of how it is conducted, have costs to everyone involved including the children who may inadvertently be trafficked. We do not think intended parents set out to become criminals or harm the children that are born of illegal surrogacy arrangements but some are prepared to act recklessly enough for the result to be the same. The women who act as surrogates in these circumstances are sometimes victims themselves but no one wants to look too closely at their situation. Society does pay a price for requiring altruistic surrogacy.

The biggest cost, however, is to the surrogate or donor in perfectly legal settings. The situation of egg donors is revealing. Anna Curtis (2010) conducted research with egg donors in the US, similar to that done by Berend with surrogates. Although the egg donors were paid, and the procedures conducted through commercial agencies and clinics, the dominant theme for the women was altruistic motivation. Curtis argues that the 'rhetoric of altruism is gendered in such a way that women are expected to be emotionally invested in the families they donate to' (Curtis 2010: 80). Egg donation is risky but focussing on the needs of the recipient rather than their own health meant that the women put aside the risks they were running while they conformed to the ideals of 'motherhood' and 'sacrifice'. As we have seen with surrogacy, the recipients also expected their donors to want to help and to care about them, without permitting them to make any 'reciprocal demands'. All financial motivation had to be suppressed, not just in their profiles, from which the recipients were choosing, but in themselves. Curtis maintains that allowing only one motivation, whether it is financial or altruistic, is detrimental and egg donors should be able to express both. She thinks that if they could openly reflect on whether they were being paid adequately for the risks they were taking they might make better decisions, ones that gave proper consideration to their own interests.

Gendering

Altruism and gift-giving are gendered across a wide range of activities from Christmas giving, where women spend more on gifts for friends than men do and also on gifts for people in 'more distant network layers' (Dyble et al. 2015: 143), to 'unpaid task assistance' (Ashwin et al. 2013). The tasks that women were most likely to undertake in a Russian study were child care for their grandchildren and care of elder members of the family. The women's assistance was seen 'as a naturally arising obligation rather than as a gift requiring reciprocation.' (Ashwin et al. 2013: 401). Several features of the women's situation are similar to those of surrogates. The assistance they provided was costly as they gave significant time to demanding work and gave up opportunities for paid labour; reciprocation was unlikely because their assistance was less valued than men's; and they could not easily respond to non-reciprocation by ceasing to provide care because they were emotionally invested in it.

Women's work, particularly care and nurture, is not seen as real work. It belongs to the home sphere rather than the public sphere. Jessica Peet (2016) argues that the reproductive economy, where women are inevitably located in ways that men are not, is not recognized in the way the productive economy is so all the work that women do in it is devalued. This is the case even when the work is paid and businesses exist that clearly are part of the productive economy. Peet (2016: 171–189) is doubly concerned about the case of transnational surrogacy because not only are women having their work devalued because they are women, they are also subject to the devaluation associated with race and class.

Altruistic self-sacrifice is expected of women and taken for granted. It is not expected of men and when it occurs it is praised and duly rewarded. Although it is difficult to eradicate the gendering effects of women's care work, better concepts than altruism are available that encompass the moral qualities needed for surrogacy and other care work, and also for the appropriate moral response from recipients of that care.

Generosity

Altruism as an ideal does appalling damage to individuals trying to help others. Society bears the cost of a deeply flawed approach to vitally important areas of human welfare. We argue that none of this harm is necessary and we propose a radical revision of the central value in surrogacy by replacing altruism with generosity. In donation of all kinds: blood, gametes and organs, the same change would greatly improve the treatment of both donors and recipients. In the caring professions, the removal of altruism in favour of generosity would ease the burden for practitioners who already struggle with the demanding nature of their work. If we replace altruism with generosity as a central value in surrogacy we can provide a better account of action undertaken for the benefit of others in all the areas where altruism is currently used. In some of the literature, generosity and altruism are used almost interchangeably, but generosity is a distinct concept even if it shares some characteristics with altruism. It is also a less difficult one to define and apply.

Generosity is 'giving more than expected, out of the goodness of one's heart' (Sablosky 2014: 547). To be generous 'we give with the intention of benefiting the recipient, out of a concern for his or her welfare.' (Kupfer 1998: 357). It provides 'a benefit which is not due another because of duty, obligation, or desert.' (Kupfer 1998: 359). The benefit that generous people give is something that they value and 'the more we value what we give, the more generous we are.' (Kupfer 1998: 358). This is where generosity touches altruism, when it is understood sociologically as 'behavior that benefits other people at a cost to oneself.' (Sablosky 2014: 549). However, it is clear that generosity has a moral quality that altruism need not have and it brings together the two apparently contradictory elements of gift-giving, altruism and self-interest.

Generosity and Self-interest

Unlike altruism, generosity is not in conflict with self-interest. Giving more than is owed does not have to be done at the expense of one's financial security or providing for one's own needs. Giving up spare time to volunteer at a charity is generous, as is giving money that would have been spent on pleasure. While we might praise people whose generosity is sacrificial in some way, we do not say that there is something tainted or suspect about minimal generosity in the way that people do about impure altruism. To compensate someone for undertaking an arduous, generous course of action—keeping in mind that no one has a duty to donate an organ or carry someone's baby—does not stop it being generous. It merely allows the person to meet their own legitimate needs.

To understand how generosity functions in human lives we need to turn to anthropology, sociology and psychology. These are the disciplines that should inform an ethical account of generosity. The harm that comes to people when psychologically impossible demands are made of them, as we saw with 'pure altruism', must be avoided. The best way to do that is not to make psychologically impossible demands. Generosity is already part of our moral landscape. We recognize it when we see it and it does not have to pass a test: generous people do not have to prove that they are generous in the way that we currently expect proof of altruistic motivation. But more importantly, we know what the proper response to generosity is: gratitude, acknowledgement, reciprocation. The two qualities, generosity and gratitude, operating together, provide the moral framework for relational activities, such as donation, surrogacy and care.

Generosity at Work

There is no contradiction in the claim that paid professionals can be generous in the way they do their work. Michelle Brock et al. (2016) found that generous clinicians, whose prosocial preferences had been identified in a laboratory experiment, provided significantly better care to their patients than ungenerous ones. They used the list of protocols clinicians were expected to follow in each patient consultation as their measure of care. Fulfilment of each part of the protocol was more arduous for the clinician in both time and effort. The generous clinicians were much more likely to complete the protocol than the ungenerous ones. However, valuable as it is to have generous professionals who carry out all the tasks related to the care they provide rather than do the minimum they can get away with, such considerations do not exhaust the possibilities of generosity. Generosity is a rich concept.

Dimensions of Generosity

Joseph Kupfer (1998) identifies two dimensions of generosity: corporeal generosity and generosity of spirit. Anything material or economic that we give is a form of corporeal generosity but what resonates most in the current context is the giving of embodied selves. Obviously donation of blood and organs are acts of corporeal generosity and it dominates in surrogacy, but the care provided by professionals whose work is physically demanding is also corporeal generosity. Child care, patient care, elder care, teaching and social work, to name just a few, take a physical toll on individuals. However, it is also work that cannot be done well without generosity of spirit.

There are two ways of showing generosity of spirit: generous-mindedness and generous-heartedness. Generous-mindedness involves making 'a favorable judgment', giving people the benefit of the doubt, interpreting their actions in as positive a light as possible and overlooking faults rather than seeking them out (Kupfer 1998: 359). It does not require blindness to faults or dishonest appraisals that will lead to harm.

Generous-heartedness is 'emotional giving' (Kupfer 1998: 360). Forgiveness, putting aside resentment and doing so out of 'good will or compassion' is generous-hearted. So is identification with others. Empathy and seeing matters from others' point of view can be generous-hearted. Generosity of spirit enables people to 'perform duties graciously' and to incur extra obligations (Kupfer 1998: 363).

Such generosity can also lead to a 'delight' in being generous. Far from being suspicious of people who take pleasure in giving, we should take it as a marker of generosity unless we have reason to think otherwise. Generally speaking, we want people to enjoy doing morally good things. The provision of care as well as surrogacy and donation are not exceptions.

Anne Arber and Ann Gallagher (2009) show how generosity of spirit can operate in the practice of nursing. Generous-hearted nurses will 'forgive people who have been disrespectful, difficult, aggressive or violent towards them' (Arber and Gallagher 2009: 777). Again, we would caution against taking this to extremes, but, in conjunction with generous-mindedness, care can be given with more empathy if nurses are generous-hearted. The particular case they use is a team meeting regarding a patient in palliative care whose pain they struggle to control. The consultant describes the patient as 'aggressive when in pain', 'demanding', 'fed-up' and writing letters of complaint. The chaplain and nurse consistently reinterpret these negative and accusatory judgements. To them, the patient is 'anxious and worried' and his behaviour normal given the circumstances. They display 'empathetic maturity', which is 'how the self understands the personhood of another' (Arber and Gallagher 2009: 781).

Gratitude

The type of generosity described above is what all of us desire when we are vulnerable and in need of care. It is appropriate for all community sharing gift relationships but it must not be unidirectional. The recipient of generosity should be grateful. Gratitude is a complex concept but an indispensable one.

The literature on gratitude in philosophy and psychology is extensive, with many different conceptions of what gratitude is and how it functions. Liz Gulliford et al. (2013) canvas some of the debate, including whether gratitude is a moral virtue, an emotion, a dyadic or triadic concept, a stable character trait that can enhance wellbeing, and more. Fortunately, we do not have to decide on most of these issues because we are looking at a very specific context for gratitude, the features of which are not controversial. Gratitude as a response to generosity requires only that there be a benefactor and a real or intended benefit of value to the recipient. We think that intended benefits as well as real benefits should be included in our analysis because in surrogacy, donation and care, the risk of failure is high. The surrogate might have a miscarriage, the organ might be rejected or the carer be unable to relieve her patient's symptoms. In those circumstances 'thank you for trying' seems the appropriate response. In each of these contexts the gratitude called for could come from a settled disposition or be an episodic emotion or even be without accompanying feelings. Whichever account of the underlying nature of gratitude turns out to be correct, its function in this context is unaffected. Similarly, whether gratitude is a general moral duty or not, there are clearly some settings in which it is morally required. Amy Mullin (2011) thinks that recipients of caring labour, when it is done with the right sort of respect for them, should be grateful to the carers. Recipients of generosity, which is not something that is owed to them, then, should be grateful to the benefactor.

It is not unreasonable to expect the intended parents to express gratitude and recognize that they owe their surrogate gratitude. Gratitude fits the context of community sharing relationships perfectly. In psychology these relationships are referred to as communal relations. Participants in these relationships who find that reciprocation is not possible or not expected or could be delayed recognize that gratitude is the appropriate response for those situations. In market pricing relationships, by contrast, feelings of gratitude are not triggered (Simão and Seibt 2014).

The Functions of Gratitude

Gratitude has certain functions within social relationships, summarized by Sara Algoe (2012) as 'find, remind and bind.' Expressions of gratitude can act as a signal to someone that there is a potential relationship available (find), they can remind partners of the fact that this is an important relationship, and they bring the partners closer together (bind). The effect of expressions of gratitude on the benefactor is positive. They report more satisfaction with the relationship, though with one important caveat. If the benefactor thinks the expression of gratitude shows low responsiveness, they do not report increased satisfaction (Algoe and Zhaoyang 2016). In a test of the 'find' element of the theory, Lisa Williams and Monica Bartlett (2015) report that the perceived warmth of the expression of gratitude influenced the benefactor's decision about whether to pursue the relationship. Clearly there are limits to what an expression of gratitude can accomplish. In what follows we show why generosity and gratitude are central values in the professional model of surrogacy.

Gratitude and Generosity in the Professional Model

Surrogates are generous when they undertake to carry a baby for someone else. No one has a duty to be a surrogate. Their corporeal generosity is obvious but, given the nature of the relationship, they are also generous-hearted. In a community sharing gift relationship the benefactor gives emotionally, identifies with the recipient and displays empathy. This is what the intended parents want from their surrogate (Murphy 2015). The benefactor typically gives care or services for which no direct form of reciprocation is possible and this feature signals to the recipient that gratitude is the appropriate response. A baby has neither price nor equivalent to be given in return. Gratitude is called for. In fact, in the case we cited above, Tessa's intended father was entirely wrong: he had everything to be grateful for. Thanks to Tessa he and his wife had their family. But her generosity was completely overlooked.

There are also many occasions for surrogates to be generous-minded. The path to surrogacy for infertile couples is often one of heartbreak, with failed IVF, miscarriages and increasing despair. Surrogacy launches them on another uncertain journey as attempts to establish a pregnancy through IVF are frequently unsuccessful and surrogates can decide not to keep trying. When a pregnancy is established, the surrogate faces all the normal risks associated with it. In addition to those, the intended parents in most jurisdictions have to overcome obstacles in order to be acknowledged as the legal parents. It is immensely stressful and this can affect the way they relate to the surrogate. The surrogate who can see them as 'anxious and worried' rather than 'aggressive,' hostile, or controlling and can understand their behaviour is generous-minded. However, she should not tolerate actual aggression or the sort of control that some intended parents attempt to exert (Teman 2010).

When the intended parents recognize the surrogate's generosity towards them, the required response is gratitude. Gratitude has the functions outlined above but we also think it is useful in orienting the intended parents to their obligations towards the surrogate. Gratitude encourages respectful treatment, consideration of her needs, an honoured place in their family history and acknowledgement of her desire to be kept informed of the child's progress. It precludes unreasonable demands before, during and after the process. It precludes relational devaluation when she is no longer useful to them. The relationship inevitably changes but it should change in a way that is acceptable to both parties.

It is obvious that no one can make the intended parents feel grateful. If they are less grateful than they should be then the surrogate is likely to find the response unsatisfactory. These are psychological facts that we do not attempt to avoid or dismiss. However, the professional model provides a context that encourages grateful behaviour, such as regular updates on the baby's progress. Of course, we cannot eliminate the risk that the intended parents will eventually stop contact with the surrogate when she wishes it to continue, but a great deal can be done to reduce this risk.

The professional model takes the nature of the relationship as the foundation on which to build the necessary ethical structure. A community sharing gift relationship defines the sort of obligations that arise for the surrogates and intended parents. The surrogate's generosity is a given, and the intended parents' obligations towards her are not negotiable. Because the nature of the arrangement is wholly transparent and unambiguous the intended parents are no longer able to change the rules as it suits them. But the intended parents also know that the surrogate cannot change the rules either and, with the legal provisions advocated in Chap. 5, certainty over parentage is guaranteed from the beginning.

The adversarial potential of the commercial model, which is the means for resolving conflicts in market pricing relationships, does not exist in the professional model. The professional model provides regulatory oversight and mechanisms for the resolution of disputes. Whatever goes wrong, recourse to the courts will not be necessary. There is no longer any expectation of altruism or self-sacrifice. Instead there are reasonable demands only.

Conclusion

Altruistic surrogacy takes altruism as its basic moral value. It is a freely given gift with no expectation of reciprocation. However, the psychological mechanism underlying it is gift exchange, which does require reciprocity. Gift exchanges establish and stabilize bonds across a wide range of activity and are part of human evolution. People intuitively expect returns and failure to reciprocate may signal that the giver is not highly valued. Gift relationships come in distinct forms, community sharing and market pricing being the most relevant to surrogacy. In commercial surrogacy the intended parents tend to believe they are in a market pricing relationship. They view payment to the surrogate as all they are required to give her because it is only a business transaction. By contrast, despite getting paid, commercial surrogates tend to respond to the community sharing aspects of the relationship and, therefore, risk relational devaluation. Surrogates are expected to identify with the needs of the intended parents at the expense of their own and to be motivated by altruism even in commercial arrangements.

We argued that gift language is problematic, particularly in altruistic surrogacy. Surrogacy and organ donation share the 'gift of life' metaphor, which is linked to altruism. They are expected to give a pure gift, unsullied by rewards. This imposes significant costs on donors and recipients. It fails to recognize the sacrifice donors make and recipients feel burdened by a gift they can never repay. Donors' own legitimate needs are not taken into account. Surrogates are in the same predicament. Any claim they make for themselves sullies the altruistic nature of their gift.

Instead of altruism, we proposed that the moral value most appropriate to surrogacy is generosity. Generosity is giving more than is owed, whether that is through material giving or the generous spirit with which work is done. It does not require self-sacrifice and is compatible with payment. Because surrogacy is never a duty, compensating the surrogate does not change the fact that it is a generous thing to do. She can have her own legitimate needs taken into account. Generosity also allows reciprocity. The proper response to generosity is gratitude. The relationship between intended parents and surrogate is closest to being a community sharing one and policy should reflect that. In a community sharing relationship, such as surrogacy, generosity and gratitude are the values that best capture the moral nature of the undertaking.

While generosity rather than altruism is an essential moral concept in the professional model, it is not the only one. Relationships need to be based on trust. In the next chapter we examine the nature of trust and how it functions in relationships. No model for the regulation of surrogacy will succeed without a good understanding of trust.

References

Algoe, S. B. (2012). Find, remind, and bind: The functions of gratitude in everyday relationships. *Social and Personality Psychology Compass, 6*(6), 455–469.

Algoe, S. B., & Zhaoyang, R. (2016). Positive psychology in context: Effects of expressing gratitude in ongoing relationships depend on perceptions of enactor responsiveness. *The Journal of Positive Psychology, 11*(4), 399–415.

Arber, A., & Gallagher, A. (2009). Generosity and the moral imagination in the practice of teamwork. *Nursing Ethics, 16*(6), 775–785.

Ashwin, S., Tartakovskaya, I., Ilyina, M., & Lytkina, T. (2013). Gendering reciprocity: Solving a puzzle of nonreciprocation. *Gender & Society, 27*(3), 396–421.

Berend, Z. (2012). The romance of surrogacy. *Sociological Forum, 27*(4), 913–936.

Berend, Z. (2014). The social context for surrogates' motivations and satisfaction. *Reproductive BioMedicine Online, 29*(4), 399–401.

Bishop, J. P., & Rees, C. E. (2007). Hero or has-been: Is there a future for altruism in medical education? *Advances in Health Sciences Education, 12*(3), 391–399.

Brock, J. M., Lange, A., & Leonard, K. L. (2016). Generosity and prosocial behavior in healthcare provision: Evidence from the laboratory and field. *Journal of Human Resources, 51*(1), 133–162.

Crowley-Matoka, M., & Hamdy, S. F. (2016). Gendering the gift of life: Family politics and kidney donation in Egypt and Mexico. *Medical Anthropology, 35*(1), 31–44.

Curtis, A. (2010). Giving 'til it hurts: Egg donation and the costs of altruism. *Feminist Formations, 22*(2), 80–100.

Dufner, A. (2015). Blood products and the commodification debate: The blurry concept of altruism and the 'implicit price' of readily available body parts. *HEC Forum, 27*(4), 347–359.

Dyble, M., van Leeuwen, A. J., & Dunbar, R. I. M. (2015). Gender differences in Christmas gift-giving. *Evolutionary Behavioral Sciences, 9*(2), 140–144.

Fortin, M.-C., Dion-Labrie, M., Hébert, M.-J., & Doucet, H. (2010). The enigmatic nature of altruism in organ transplantation: A cross-cultural study of transplant physicians' views on altruism. *BMC Research Notes, 3*(1), 216.

Gulliford, L., Morgan, B., & Kristjánsson, K. (2013). Recent work on the concept of gratitude in philosophy and psychology. *Journal of Value Inquiry, 47*(3), 285–317.

Komter, A. (2007). Gifts and social relations: The mechanisms of reciprocity. *International Sociology, 22*(1), 93–107.

Komter, A. (2010). The evolutionary origins of human generosity. *International Sociology, 25*(3), 443–464.

Kupfer, J. (1998). Generosity of spirit. *The Journal of Value Inquiry, 32*(3), 357–368.

Lemay, E. P., Jr., Overall, N. C., & Clark, M. S. (2012). Experiences and interpersonal consequences of hurt feelings and anger. *Journal of Personality and Social Psychology, 103*(6), 982–1006.

Lemmergaard, J., & Muhr, S. L. (2011). Regarding gifts—on Christmas gift exchange and asymmetrical business relations. *Organization, 18*(6), 763–777.

Mullin, A. (2011). Gratitude and caring labor. *Ethics and Social Welfare, 5*(2), 110–122.

Murphy, D. (2015). *Gay men pursuing parenthood through surrogacy: Reconfiguring kinship.* Sydney: University of New South Wales Press.

Pande, A. (2009). "It may be her eggs but it's my blood": Surrogates and everyday forms of kinship in India. *Qualitative Sociology, 32*(4), 379–397.

Pande, A. (2014). *Wombs in labor: Transnational commercial surrogacy in India.* New York: Columbia University Press.

Peet, J. L. (2016). A womb that is (not always) one's own. *International Feminist Journal of Politics, 18*(2), 1–19.

Pennings, G. (2015). Central role of altruism in the recruitment of gamete donors. *Monash Bioethics Review, 33*(1), 78–88.

Pettersen, T. (2012). Conceptions of care: Altruism, feminism, and mature care. *Hypatia, 27*(2), 366–389.

Sablosky, R. (2014). Does religion foster generosity? *The Social Science Journal, 51*(4), 545–555.

Saunders, B. (2012). Altruism or solidarity? The motives for organ donation and two proposals. *Bioethics, 26*(7), 376–381.

Scheper-Hughes, N. (2007). The tyranny of the gift: Sacrificial violence in living donor transplants. *American Journal of Transplantation, 7*(3), 507–511.

Shaw, R. (2010). Perceptions of the gift relationship in organ and tissue donation: Views of intensivists and donor and recipient coordinators. *Social Science & Medicine, 70*(4), 609–615.

Shaw, R. (2012). Thanking and reciprocating under the New Zealand organ donation system. *Health, 16*(3), 298–313.

Shaw, R., & Webb, R. (2015). Multiple meanings of "gift" and its value for organ donation. *Qualitative Health Research, 25*(5), 600–611.

Shaw, R. M., & Bell, L. J. M. (2015). 'Because you can't live on love': Living kidney donors' perspectives on compensation and payment for organ donation. *Health Expectations, 18*(6), 3201–3212.

Shearmur, J. (2015). Koplin, Titmuss and the social tail that wags the dog. *Monash Bioethics Review, 33*(2), 123–129.

Simão, C., & Seibt, B. (2014). Gratitude depends on the relational model of communal sharing. *PLoS ONE, 9*(1), e86158.

Siminoff, L. A., & Chillag, K. (1999). The fallacy of the "gift of life". *The Hastings Center Report, 29*(6), 34–41.

Steinberg, D. (2010). Altruism in medicine: Its definition, nature, and dilemmas. *Cambridge Quarterly of Healthcare Ethics, 19*(02), 249–257.

Teman, E. (2010). *Birthing a mother: The surrogate body and the pregnant self.* Berkeley: University of California Press.

Williams, L. A., & Bartlett, M. Y. (2015). Warm thanks: Gratitude expression facilitates social affiliation in new relationships via perceived warmth. *Emotion, 15*(1), 1–5.

4

Trustworthiness and Care

Introduction

Successful surrogacy relationships depend on mutual trust. Unfortunately trust is frequently absent or is undermined by events in the course of the relationship because there is no adequate basis for building it. Intended parents worry about whether they can really trust the surrogate, who is in turn worried about whether she can really trust them to carry out their commitments to her and the baby. In this chapter we draw on the literature in psychology and management to explain what trust is and how it works. Although there are cultural variations in the way trust is built up between people, research shows that the mechanism underlying these practices is the same across cultures. We will focus on the two most commonly recognized forms of trust, namely relational and calculative trust. Failure to understand the distinctive processes underlying each of them leads to difficulties in surrogacy relationships. We also examine how differences in power and status affect trust. We then demonstrate how the structure of the caring professions enables them to accommodate both types of trust and enhance the trustworthiness of practitioners. We draw an analogy between professional

© The Author(s) 2017
R. Walker and L. van Zyl, *Towards a Professional Model of Surrogate Motherhood*,
DOI 10.1057/978-1-137-58658-2_4

trust and trust in surrogacy, and then explain the similarities between professional care and gestational care.

What Is Trust?

In surrogacy relationships it is the intended parents who give trust first. This initial trust is the focus of our examination of the concept of trust. Once a surrogacy relationship is established, both parties have to trust each other, but the relationship only exists because the intended parents first put their trust in a surrogate. We will bring back the Allbrights and Bandini to help explain what is going on when people put their trust in someone.

We all know that trust is crucial in every type of relationship. Although it is easy to notice when it is absent, the nature of trust is harder to grasp. The literature on trust is vast but there is broad support for certain basic elements of trust. Here is a simple description of what happens. The Allbrights make a decision to trust Bandini because they think that she intends to carry out their wishes and will not let them down. This makes them vulnerable because she could fail them. Their belief that she will behave as they desire could be wrong. So we have the three core features of trust: vulnerability, positive expectations of another and an intention to act on these expectations (Rousseau et al. 1998). However, there are important differences between the two types of trust we consider. A failure to recognize these differences leads people to make mistakes in their decision-making about whom to trust and with what.

Calculative Trust

Calculative trust is the form of trust we are most familiar with in market pricing relationships. If the Allbrights trust Bandini in this way, they would deliberate and think their way through all the costs and benefits of the decision to use Bandini's services. They would assess whether the benefits were greater than the costs.

Certain risks come with every decision to embark on surrogacy. They might not be able to establish a viable pregnancy, Bandini could have a miscarriage, or they could run out of money before they succeed in having a baby. The Allbrights would also consider how likely it is that Bandini herself will betray their trust. They may well decide to use Bandini precisely because there is much less risk of a surrogate in the developing world being able to defraud them or refuse to relinquish the baby. Nevertheless they would attempt to assess the probability of every foreseeable risk and try to reduce those risks with conditions in the contract. This is the purpose of contractual safeguards. For those safeguards to work the Allbrights have to be able to assess the risks accurately and the safeguards have to be feasible (Braynov 2013; James 2014; Poppo et al. 2016; Williamson 1993).

Relational Trust

Much more familiar to us is the trust we put in people in our everyday lives. Relational or interpersonal trust involves different processes from those that underpin calculative trust and is usually built up over the course of interactions between people. But the same processes also drive the trust people put in strangers. If the Allbrights trust Bandini in this way it is not the result of conscious deliberation and calculation. The relevant cognitive and emotional mechanisms work automatically and the Allbrights would not be aware of them. They might talk about feeling a connection with Bandini and feeling that she is a good person who wants to help them. The Allbrights cannot choose whether to have these feelings. In general terms that is not a bad thing. The ability to trust people almost immediately using rough rules of thumb is vital to humans as they navigate their way through a social world filled with uncertainty. There is neither time nor the ability to make complex calculations about whether to trust people in everyday situations.

Relational trust is at work where there is uncertainty, that is, where risks cannot be quantified and safeguards cannot be put in place. The Allbrights trust Bandini because they feel she is trustworthy even though they cannot know whether she really is a good person who wants to do the right thing. No one can ever be certain that another person is morally good, but in community sharing relationships, this is the assumption we all make (Braynov 2013; James 2014; Poppo et al. 2016).

Risk and Uncertainty

Although risk and uncertainty tend to be treated as the same thing, or aspects of the same thing, they are distinct from each other. A risk can be quantified, that is, assigned a probability that can be factored into calculations. Uncertainty, by contrast, cannot be quantified. If we cannot, in principle, specify the probability of a possible outcome then it is an uncertainty. For example, the risk of a failed attempt at IVF is something the Allbrights could assign a probability to because there is good evidence of the success rates. They could then plan either to reduce the risk by implanting multiple embryos or to work out how many attempts they can afford to have, based on the number of attempts likely to be needed before they succeed. However, there is also some uncertainty for them. They cannot know what Bandini herself will choose to do. She is an independent being with her own intentions and desires. People's intentions, objectives, beliefs and moral principles are hidden from others and sometimes from themselves. The Allbrights might say that it is unlikely that Bandini will change her mind or refuse to do something in the contract but this is based on subjective assessment. They cannot effectively safeguard themselves from this uncertainty.

Trustworthiness

The Allbrights decide to make that first move and trust Bandini. Why? The answer might seem obvious or facetious but it is not. They think that Bandini is trustworthy. Their decision is based on a perception of trustworthiness and could be wrong. The perception can come from a number of sources and these differ according to whether it is relational or calculative trust. We will begin with the latter.

The Allbrights could trust Bandini because they think it is in her interests to be trustworthy. Their contract with her could have provisions that make it worth her while not to betray their trust. As we saw above, the role of contractual safeguards is to reduce risk. If they work well, Bandini will be more likely to cooperate with the Allbrights if one of the foreseeable risks actually occurs. She might miscarry, for example, but be willing to try again because the Allbrights have ensured that she will be suitably rewarded for doing so. In that way safeguards can increase trustworthiness. They work particularly well when the person who has to trust does not know a great deal about the person she is trusting. The Allbrights do not know much about Bandini because they have only just encountered each other. She is in another country and they will almost certainly struggle to communicate with her directly. They will have to rely on the contract to encourage trustworthy behaviour. This type of strategy to enhance trustworthiness works best in business relationships (Schilke and Cook 2015).

Ideally, when anyone enters into an agreement that requires trust they will know quite a lot about the person they are trusting. There are a number of ways to acquire that information. The Allbrights could seek out a clinic that has a good reputation (Schilke and Cook 2015). If Bandini is based at a clinic with a good track record of successful surrogacies and ethical conduct towards its clients the Allbrights could be more confident because the clinic has a very strong interest in maintaining its reputation. It does not want clients to be reporting to the media that they were defrauded or that the baby was unhealthy because of their practices or that illicit behaviour by the clinic led to difficulties taking the baby home with them. These are the sort of things that put clinics out of business and bring down the wrath of their own government on them. If the Allbrights are able to rely on the clinic's reputation they will not have to use costly safeguards. The clinic's reputation reduces risk and they do not have to find other ways to protect themselves from the same risks.

If we consider perceptions of trustworthiness from a relational perspective there is one very important source of information: familiarity. Whether it is a personal relationship or a business one, familiarity with the values of the partner enables the person or business to assess trustworthiness. Shared values and goals increase perceived trustworthiness (Schilke and Cook 2015: 278). However, it takes time and a history of interactions to gain this familiarity. The Allbrights do not have this history with Bandini or the clinic. They do not know if Bandini does have the same values they have and, realistically, they do not have a way of finding out. Compare this with an alternative scenario.

Suppose the Allbrights had a lifelong friend, Bethany, who offered to be their surrogate. Over the course of their friendship they have learned about Bethany's values, reliability and approach to tasks she does for others. She and they identify with each other and Bethany knows how desperately they want a child. They have a strong bond. People in long-established relationships very often find that trust increases over time. If they have not made a mistake early on by trusting too much, this is likely to happen. The longer the Allbrights have known Bethany the more they trust her. Unless they trusted her too much to begin with and find out over time that she was less trustworthy than they thought, time gives them confidence (Vanneste et al. 2014). Friends or family members do not always make the best surrogates but sometimes they do. Let us assume that Bethany would make a good surrogate for the Allbrights but that she is unavailable.

With Bandini the Allbrights are in danger of being undermined by the automatic processes that generate relational trust. They have a real bond with Bethany that was formed over time. However, they could make an instantly favourable judgement of Bandini and feel they have a similar bond with her. They know that Bethany is trustworthy but they do not know that Bandini is because they do not have a history with her. They have only a perception her of trustworthiness that feels the same as their perception of Bethany's trustworthiness.

It is actual trustworthiness that matters. The Allbrights are in an exchange relationship with Bandini and in any exchange relationship the person who trusts is vulnerable in a very particular way. The Allbrights are vulnerable to Bandini acting in a self-seeking or opportunistic way. Instead of serving the Allbrights' interests she could serve her own (Schilke and Cook 2015). In both altruistic and commercial surrogacy, the trustors (that is, the intended parents) are vulnerable to opportunistic behaviour by the surrogate, such as a refusal to relinquish the baby or having a termination against their wishes. If the surrogate does either of these things she betrays their positive expectations of her behaviour and intentions.

Trust

The two current models of surrogacy appear to be relying on different forms of trust. The altruistic model depends on relational trust, while the commercial model is based on calculative trust. In altruistic surrogacy the intended parents' expectations rest on the bond of shared values and goals. They assume that the surrogate will not act opportunistically because she identifies with their desires. Their desires are also her desires. In commercial surrogacy, the contract, with its safeguards of controls and incentives, is meant to reduce the risk of opportunistic behaviour.

However, it is misleading to think that calculative and relational trust are alternative ways to trust. We think that the unexamined assumption of the current models of surrogacy is that only relational trust is relevant to altruistic surrogacy and only calculative trust is relevant to commercial surrogacy. If that is the case, then it is a mistake that has consequences in both forms of surrogacy arrangement. People cannot separate the different types of trust because the external environment in which all human interactions take place contains both risk and uncertainty. This means that both calculative and relational factors will be at work. In addition, research in psychology indicates that human cognition is set up so that people respond to relational cues while they are doing calculations. They could be quite unaware of doing this, but it will affect their decision to trust.

The External Environment

All decisions to trust are made in an environment external to the person who trusts. The features of the environment show that both types of trust are always involved. To see how, it is useful to consider a claim by

Oliver Williamson (1993), namely that calculative trust is not real trust. He argues that someone who has put safeguards in place against knowable risks is not vulnerable to betrayal. When the Allbrights factored in the probability of failed attempts at IVF or made provisions in case Bandini could not continue, they could not be betrayed because they had eliminated real vulnerability. If Bandini decided that she could not manage another attempt then they would implement their alternative plan, which might be to use another surrogate from that clinic. They could not be harmed by losing Bandini because a real betrayal involves more than a foreseeable financial cost. They would be facing additional outlay for further attempts and they could be disappointed if Bandini had to give up but they could not be truly surprised and shocked by the outcome. The harm would not amount to a moral loss (James 2014). For that to happen there has to be uncertainty, that is, unknowable outcomes that the Allbrights could not safeguard against. If the environment consisted only of quantifiable risks Williamson could be right. But it appears that no such environments exist, which means that intended parents are always vulnerable to betrayal.

We have already seen that the Allbrights face uncertainty with Bandini because they do not know what her intentions are. That is not just because they do not know her. They would face uncertainty with Bethany too, because what happens in the minds of others, including their moral dispositions, is inherently inaccessible. But their motivations and moral values are crucial to their trustworthiness. However well the Allbrights know Bethany, they have access only to what she says and does. That can only ever be part of the evidence for her trustworthiness. Potentially, then, in any environment people can be betrayed by someone turning out to be untrustworthy. As a result they are always vulnerable to opportunistic behaviour because all environments contain both risk and uncertainty. It is very easy to be wrong about the 'internal dispositions' of another person (James 2014). There will always be factors that cannot be quantified and cannot be safeguarded against. Decisions to trust require very complex judgements, some of which can only be made on subjective grounds.

Incentives to foster trustworthiness work up to a point and it is prudent to use them, but they can never amount to constant surveillance of the sort that would be needed to guarantee trustworthy behaviour. Not only is monitoring expensive and potentially counterproductive, it risks becoming unethical. The control over transnational surrogates in some clinics breaches the women's human rights. Bandini might have to endure conditions that Bethany would not tolerate. When intended parents attempt similar levels of surveillance and control in domestic surrogacy, difficulties in the relationship often ensue. The Allbrights should simply hope that Bandini is disposed to be trustworthy and leave her to act as an autonomous person. At some point in all exchange relationships the trusting party has to give their partner discretion to act (Lumineau 2014; Poppo et al. 2016; Schilke and Cook 2015).

The Allbrights may find transnational surrogacy attractive because Bandini would be under constant surveillance, likely to have little freedom of movement and few opportunities to make decisions they would oppose. Before we condemn them for that it is worth thinking about some of the uncertainties intended parents face regardless of the type of surrogacy arrangement they have. Some of the most important decisions about the pregnancy rest on the moral dispositions of the surrogate. Will she keep her promise to abstain from alcohol? Will she share information with them? Will she relinquish the baby or even carry the pregnancy to term? The uncertainties are greater in domestic surrogacy. Even if the Allbrights did have Bethany as their surrogate, uncertainties would remain because Bethany herself might not know in advance what she would do when faced with a particularly grave decision. For example, there is a quantifiable risk of fetal abnormality but the surrogate's decision to terminate or continue the pregnancy is uncertain. These are the moments when what people think they would do in the abstract can turn out to be unthinkable in practice.

Human Psychology

It is also impossible to separate calculative and relational trust because of the way people's brains and bodies function biologically. Even while people are deliberating, thinking, and calculating costs and benefits, their bodies are getting ready to act, which involves both emotional and physical responses (Braynov 2013: 12). These responses occur automatically and below the level of conscious awareness. They are also very fast. That means that people are already feeling the decision before they consciously arrive at it. Everyone thinks they are using reason alone but that is never the case. In all instances of calculative trust, there will be input from the systems involved in relational trust.

It is not necessarily a bad thing that it is impossible to disentangle calculative and relational trust. Neither is a superior form of trust and both are very valuable to humans in their own way. The unconscious responses of our brains and bodies that drive relational trust are important to humans because they are quick and low cost. They prompt us to trust strangers and to give trust spontaneously in order to take advantage of situations as they arise. The rough and ready rules might fail, but they very often succeed and we could not function socially without them. However, we do need to be concerned with the confusion that arises from failing to understand how they work, how they influence each other, the sort of mistakes people are likely to make, and what the appropriate mechanisms are for managing risk and uncertainty.

We see examples of such mistakes in surrogacy relationships when intended parents try to control for uncertainty over the moral dispositions of the surrogate by using contractual safeguards. But this is not the only source of concern. In some cases the intended parents are not calculative enough when they are selecting a surrogate and that appears to be due to the processes underlying relational trust. So we turn now to examine relational trust in more detail.

Relational Trust in Surrogacy

Surrogacy relationships are perplexing. Whether intended parents select their surrogate from a list of profiles at an agency or through an online network, they are effectively trusting a stranger who could betray that trust. Trustor vulnerability in surrogacy is immense, but surrogacy is just a particularly vivid example of a wider, puzzling phenomenon. Trusting strangers is irrational but people do it all the time. They also make mistakes, sometimes trusting too much and sometimes too little. In spite of the importance of accurate decision-making, people are prone to systematic errors of judgement.

Why do we trust strangers when things can go so seriously wrong? The simple answer is that we want to. Some researchers suggest that people trust strangers because they feel they have to, that there is a social expectation that they should even if they would rather not (Dunning et al. 2014). However, other studies show that people giving trust do so to trigger reciprocity in the person they trust. The social expectation is not that people trust, but that people are trustworthy. There is social disapproval of people who do not respond with trustworthy behaviour, that is, do not reciprocate (Bicchieri et al. 2011). These experimental results are consistent with the findings of the anthropological studies we discussed in Chap. 3.

The problems in surrogacy relationships tend to occur because intended parents trust too much, not too little. Intended parents make the decision to trust a stranger from a relational perspective even if it is commercial surrogacy where everything is done on a contractual footing. They feel a bond and they want to trust. Both arise from powerful processes they are not even aware of.

Cues

Decisions to trust are not random. The automatic mechanisms involve the use of cues to arrive at 'good enough' decisions. These cues will be based on the characteristics of the person or on the situation. The mechanisms cut out laborious and time-consuming evaluation of probability. The benefit is that they are fast and efficient, but the cost is that they can arrive at the wrong decision. The main problem is that people giving trust often choose the wrong cues. They use the ones that are easy to detect and easy to process, but these might be irrelevant to whether someone is actually trustworthy. The information that would be helpful is much harder to find and process (Evans and Krueger 2016: 17).

Suppose the Allbrights have decided not to use Bandini's services because the way she and her sister surrogates are treated by the clinic is unethical. Bethany is not available to be their surrogate so they decide on domestic surrogacy with Candace, a woman they met online and have had video chats with. What cues would they be likely to use to make that decision? The easiest information to use is information about themselves. They can easily work out what they have to gain from the arrangement and what the costs could be. But the relevant cues are about Candace. What should the Allbrights expect her to do? The most important information for a correct decision is how much temptation there is for Candace to act in a self-seeking, opportunistic way, that is, to betray their trust. The Allbrights will probably consider this to a limited extent, but mostly they will disregard it because such information is difficult to process (Evans and Krueger 2016: 17). They are unlikely to consider the situation from Candace's perspective to see what her potential gains and losses are. This very valuable situational cue is largely overlooked.

The Allbrights are more likely to pay close attention to personal cues. One of the most powerful is Candace's appearance. They could think she looks trustworthy, particularly that she has a trustworthy face. However, appearance provides no reliable evidence of trustworthiness and it is worryingly dominant in people's decision to trust. It can override useful cues, such as reputation They are also more likely to trust Candace if she belongs to their social category. If Candace is an outsider it would make the Allbrights less inclined to trust her even though membership of social groupings is irrelevant to trustworthiness. They would also be inclined to project their own trustworthiness onto Candace because information about themselves is so much easier to come by than information about her. None of this need be done consciously (Thielmann and Hilbig 2015: 256).

Even if the Allbrights did evaluate the amount of temptation Candace would have to betray their trust they might not be able to put the information to effective use. The best way to reduce temptation is to have contractual safeguards, including sanctions. If Candace knew that breaching the contract would have negative consequences for her that outweighed any advantage she might be seeking she would be far less tempted to do it (Thielmann and Hilbig 2015: 256). However, for that to work you have to have an enforceable contract. A great many intended parents are legally prevented from having such safeguards, which means that trustee temptation can be very high. Intended parents will still tend to disregard it as a cue and trust anyway.

In summary: intended parents trust a stranger, mostly because they want to. The decision to trust that particular stranger is likely to rest on irrelevant factors such as her appearance and whether she is a member of their own group. They focus mainly on their own expectations of the outcome, that is, what it means for them. They will overlook her temptation to betray that trust and do so in the likely absence of safeguards to minimize that temptation.

Trust Within the Relationship

The decision to trust marks the beginning of a trusting process (Skinner et al. 2014), which can end badly or well. When it ends badly, it could be because the decision to trust a particular person was a mistake, but there are features of trust itself that can have negative effects (Lumineau 2014). An 'overreliance on relational trust' (Zahra et al. 2006: 541) or 'over-trust' (Goel et al. 2005) can produce the same effects as a mistake. These are part of what scholars call the 'dark side' of trust.

Once the Allbrights have decided to trust Candace and enter into a relationship with her, the mechanisms underlying relational trust can still lead them astray. They can encourage overconfidence, inadequate monitoring, 'blind faith', disregard for emerging evidence of trustee untrustworthiness, complacency and an inability to adjust to changing circumstances. As a result, they could still make errors of judgement and inaccurate assessments about the state of the relationship with Candace. That increases their vulnerability to exploitation and Candace's temptation to act for her own benefit (Gargiulo and Ertug 2006; Goel et al. 2005; Lumineau 2014; Zahra et al. 2006).

The processes outlined above can lead to situations that put both the Allbrights and Candace at a disadvantage and do so in ways that they cannot easily avoid, however much they want to (Skinner et al. 2014: 209). This is because the options for exiting the arrangement are deeply unattractive. Surrogacy relationships that run into trouble put both parties in this position. Candace would be reluctant to use her options because they are either to withhold the baby or to terminate the pregnancy. The Allbrights' options are similarly unattractive once a pregnancy is established and their genetic material is growing into a baby. They have effectively given Candace a hostage. In every jurisdiction where the surrogate is the presumptive mother of that baby, the intended parents are helpless in the face of her resistance.

Trust and Transnational Surrogacy

There are other factors that have an impact on the decision to trust and its consequences. Power and status are two of the most important. The effects of power and status are the same in altruistic and commercial surrogacy but they function differently in domestic and transnational surrogacy.

The power imbalance in surrogacy relationships is a given. Intended parents have more power than surrogates for reasons to do with socio-economic status, race (often) and the effect of gendered work. Attempts to address the power imbalance often fail because scholars assume that it works the same way in all forms of surrogacy. Solutions tend to be oversimplified and some achieve more power for the surrogate in ways that increase the vulnerability of the intended parents Yehezkel Margalit (2014) thinks that the surrogate's status as legal mother addresses the power imbalance. It does give her more power but it also puts the baby's interests in jeopardy and increases the intended parents' uncertainty. Payment is also put forward as a solution. Again, it addresses just one aspect of the surrogate's lack of power. We think that these attempts misfire because they do not capture the way power and status actually work in surrogacy relationships.

Power and Status

Power and status can only come into play when there is a relationship between at least two people. Not all relationships are affected by differences in power and/or status and not all of them are affected in the same way. They do not always occur together. To have social power is to have control of valued resources (Magee and Galinsky 2008: 361). The powerless depend on the powerful for access to these resources (Stevens and Fiske 2000). Status, by contrast, is subjectively determined by others. It consists of respect and admiration for the person (Magee and Galinsky 2008: 359). The greater the respect and admiration the higher the status. If respect is lost so is status. A person can have both power and high status. She could remain powerful even if she lost status because the only way to lose power is to lose control of the valued resources.

The Effects of Power

Power changes the way a person views the world and acts within it. To see how this works we return to the Allbrights and Bandini. The Allbrights are unquestionably powerful and Bandini has very little power. What difference does the Allbrights' power make to their view of the world? Compared with low-power individuals they are more likely to act and to be confident that they will get what they want. They have both a wider range of available actions and fewer obstacles in their path (Magee and Galinsky 2008). That does not mean that the Allbrights will act badly. They could use their power to do good (Sturm and Antonakis 2015). However, some other effects of power reduce the probability that they will. Their view of the world is probably more abstract and that makes them less likely to be aware of the interests of the people below them. They will tend to rely more on stereotypes and not often consider things from the perspective of their subordinates. This makes it difficult for them to understand the needs of others. They will be much more focussed on their own needs and interests. They are also more likely to think of others in terms of how useful they are to them. Instead of seeing Bandini as a person with needs and interests of her own they will tend to pay attention only to the needs and interests that coincide with theirs (Magee and Galinsky 2008). That is, they need a baby and Bandini needs money. All they will provide is money and they probably will not consider any of her other needs, especially those that would interfere with their own.

Power creates social distance between people. There is a large gulf between the Allbrights and Bandini that leads the Allbrights to have a poor understanding of what Bandini thinks of the arrangement or how she feels. They are, as a consequence, likely to be wrong about her intentions and plans. Unfortunately they are also likely to have limited empathy towards her (Smith and Magee 2015: 152–153). Power and social distance make them less likely to help her (Lammers et al. 2012: 283).

Status, however, can mitigate some of the effects of power. If the Allbrights want to be respected and admired they will have to pay some attention to Bandini and respond to some of her needs as a person (Magee and Galinsky 2008: 382). There are limits to what they can do without losing status. However, they have much more scope for exercising power without constraint in transnational surrogacy where they could be indifferent to whether Bandini and the clinic respect and admire them, especially when the arrangement is over.

If the Allbrights have personal qualities that make them act benevolently this would also be an effective way to use power for good. They might value their own integrity and moral goodness highly enough to treat Bandini well (Sturm and Antonakis 2015: 148). Without mediating factors, the effect of power on perceptions of lower power individuals, is often negative.

Powerless (relative to high power) individuals are dependent on the high-power individual for access to valued resources. By definition they lack control. This is a stressful situation to be in and the powerless use a range of strategies to manage it. One such strategy is to form a more favourable view of the powerful individual than is warranted. Low-power individuals unable to influence the outcome of the relationship tend to attribute benign motives to the person with power over them and see them as more competent than the evidence suggests. Even where they have some control over the outcome, they still tend to make overly favourable attributions. These attributions make the low-power person feel safer and enable them to see the situation as less threatening (Stevens and Fiske 2000; Weber et al. 2005).

Power and Trust

The psychological effects of power and powerlessness have a direct impact on trust. Bandini is dependent on the Allbrights and hopes that they are trustworthy. That hope leads her to attribute benevolence to them, that is, they will be good to her by showing trustworthy behaviour. She trusts based on her desire (Schilke et al. 2015). But the Allbrights have no need to attribute benevolence to Bandini because they have the power. They focus on themselves instead. They assume Bandini shares their intention to bring about the desired outcome, a healthy baby. In other words, both parties are making self-serving attributions about the other. It is a bias towards their own interests that affects their decisions to trust (Weber et al. 2005: 77). High status functions almost the same way. High-status individuals expect to be well-treated and give greater initial trust than lower status individuals do. If status is involved, the Allbrights would be more likely to see Bandini as benevolent (Lount and Pettit 2012). If power is the only factor then they would not be paying sufficient attention to Bandini to make attributions concerning her intentions.

Given that both the Allbrights and Bandini can be wrong because they have based their decisions on irrelevant cues, there is considerable potential for their power differentiated exchange to end badly. The management literature studies trust within and between organizations that have institutional resources available to them to limit the damage caused by misperceptions. Surrogacy relationships, by contrast, occur 'in the wild'. They are either directly between individuals or indirectly so through the mediation of an agency that might itself not be trustworthy. The Allbrights, as the ones to initiate trust have to navigate treacherous waters and are likely to be undermined by their own psychological processes. Not only can they end up being betrayed, they can do a lot of harm to Bandini. The ethical use of power depends on their individual qualities mediating the distance effects. Where they are present they can be very effective (Smith and Magee 2015; Sturm and Antonakis 2015). In their absence, social distance is potentially harmful.

Social Distance in Transnational Surrogacy

Transnational surrogacy does indeed show the power imbalance in action. Amrita Pande (2014) documents precisely the effects described above in her ethnography of Indian surrogates. The behaviour of the intended parents towards their surrogates demonstrates the effects of social distance. This occurs not just in India but wherever poorly regulated transnational surrogacy is practised. The intended parents' self-serving beliefs and expectations are on display in such matters as multiple embryo transfer, fetal reduction, establishing pregnancies with two or three surrogates at the same time, colluding with the poor practice of clinics that routinely use elective caesareans for convenience and also in the rejection of the surrogate following relinquishment.

One important insight from the trust and power literature is that none of this behaviour need be the result of deliberate callousness or immorality. Power changes psychological processes profoundly but not always consciously. The intended parents might not even be aware of how highly asymmetrical the relationship is. Pande notes that a few individuals do manage to overcome distance and the ploys of clinics in order to treat their surrogates fairly but, without a strong sense of others' needs, individuals will not even see the problem because they are processing the easy information: their own goals and desired outcomes.

Trust and Domestic Surrogacy

The situation is different in domestic surrogacy. If the Allbrights stay home and have Candace as their surrogate they encounter a factor known as 'buyer specificity'. Domestic surrogacy is more expensive than transnational surrogacy and there is a shortage of surrogates. These combine to increase Candace's temptation to act opportunistically. If the Allbrights were using Bandini and she chose not to continue or was unsatisfactory they would be able to switch to another surrogate at low cost. That gives Bandini an incentive to comply because she knows the Allbrights have other options available to them. At home it is rather different. By the time the Allbrights have found Candace and committed their financial resources to the arrangement, the cost of switching to another surrogate would be prohibitive even if they could find one. Given the scarcity of domestic surrogates, it is not obvious that they could and Candace would know that. The Allbrights' sunk costs keep them tied to the relationship so Candace can safely ignore incentives to perform well if her interests are better served by acting opportunistically (Poppo et al. 2016).

The cost of domestic surrogacy is high even if it is altruistic rather than commercial. Intended parents pay for IVF and any medical expenses and they have to pay all the compliance costs to ensure the arrangement is legal. Most intended parents are not particularly wealthy. They may be relatively better off than the surrogate but that does not necessarily mean they can afford many attempts at surrogacy. They often make significant financial sacrifices and might not be able to try again if the attempt fails.

The situation would be different again if the Allbrights had been able to have Bethany as their surrogate. Where there is authentic relational trust, such as one finds between close friends, the significance of buyer specificity changes and it becomes a sign of commitment (Poppo et al. 2016: 728). Bethany would see it as a commitment to her and respond accordingly. By contrast, Candace would see it as a vulnerability that could be exploited. In the absence of genuine relational trust that is exactly what it is.

It would be risky for Candace to exercise the power she has because her options are costly. She could demand (more) money and threaten to have a termination or withhold the baby. However, a termination is an invasive and unpleasant intervention that carries its own risks and if she refuses to relinquish the baby she is left with responsibility for it. Either she raises it herself or she puts it up for adoption but both are expensive and time-consuming, especially as the Allbrights would, meanwhile, be pursuing every legal avenue open to them to get the baby. Nevertheless, family court records show that numerous surrogates have indeed exercised some of their power to serve their own interests in this way.

Trusting Intended Parents

Although we have thought about power in relation to the intended parents, it is important to remember that after the initial trust has been given by the intended parents, the surrogate then has to trust them as she commits to a process that cannot be ended by a simple change of mind. Once the pregnancy is established there is no easy way out of it. Here, in transnational surrogacy particularly, the features of low-power dependence are visible. Pande's surrogates attributed high levels of benevolence to their couples, especially the intended mother, and discounted information that indicated less care for them than they hoped. Bitter disappointments and betrayals awaited some of them. Very few found themselves with empathic individuals who had a strong enough concern for others to overcome the effects of social distance. Domestic surrogates in high-income countries have recourse to a legal system that upholds their rights, a medical profession that is very clear who the patient is and what her rights as a patient are and some system of social security should she strike disaster. Transnational surrogacy is notoriously lacking in such provisions.

The effects of power must be mitigated so that both parties can have confidence in the relationship. Trust is vital to surrogacy so the intended parents' initial trust needs to be grounded in the surrogate's actual (not perceived) trustworthiness. The surrogate, in turn, has to be protected from the type of behaviour social distance fosters in intended parents. To achieve these aims we need to look at how trust functions in the professions.

Trust in the Professions

All trusting relationships have calculative and relational dimensions and most involve a degree of mutual trust For them to function well they must be structured along lines that recognize and accommodate the different processes at work and the varying needs of the people in them. As we have shown, neither of the current models of surrogacy do this well. However, there is a third way of approaching the problem.

The professions, as described in Chap. 1, have trust as a core component. We now turn to the way the caring professions in particular organize themselves to provide a framework in which trust can be given safely and effectively. We focus on the caring professions and then relate their approach to trust and care to the practice of surrogacy. In these professions, the service that patients or clients trust practitioners to provide is care of one form or another. They have, accordingly, ethical values that support that aim. As we explore these values and the way they are implemented we will show their relevance to surrogacy and how using an analogous structure would make the trusting relationship safer for everyone.

First we examine the concept of care and then we show how care, trust and the professions connect to create an ethically strong basis for assisting people when they are at their most vulnerable. We then apply the results to surrogacy. To promote a professional model of surrogacy is not to turn surrogacy into a profession. Many features of professional structure, such as extensive training and supervised practice, are irrelevant. We do not think that surrogates should be making a career out of having babies for people. Women who act as surrogates do, however, provide care, and should have the professional's attitude and ethical commitment. We begin with care.

What Is Care?

Some of the common assumptions about care that people make in everyday life have to be set aside in this context in order to understand the concept of care as it applies in professional life. In this setting, care is about the provision or practice of care. The most counterintuitive aspect of such care is that it is not a feeling. Care can be accompanied by feelings, and it often is, but it does not have to be. It is not something that women are naturally better at than men. It is not every woman's vocation but neither can any member of society, male or female, escape certain basic obligations that require them to care. Regardless of their gender, every member of the caring professions knows that, while care is sometimes personally fulfilling, it can also be a burden. When people are prepared to undertake caring that they could have avoided, and they do it well, their action is praiseworthy. Yet in the short history of surrogacy, far from admiring women who volunteer to be surrogates, there has been a desperate search for some pathology to explain their abnormality, their desire to do something so 'unnatural.' In the following sections we show why this attitude is mistaken and why surrogates should be accorded much more respect than they currently receive.

Dimensions of Care

To show how care is not necessarily emotional, Stephanie Collins (2015) distinguishes between 'caring about', which refers to attitudes and emotions, and 'caring for', which refers to actions people take to provide care. She also narrows the focus to consider only morally valuable caring attitudes and actions, which she identifies as pertaining to persons (or things, theoretically) that have interests. Her account is directly relevant to the caring professions and surrogacy. She says 'We can *care about* something—pay attention to it, emotionally invest in it, worry about it. We can *care for* something—tend to it, nurture it, help it to thrive.' (Collins 2015: 49) [italics in original] Attitude and action can separate. The desperately tired nurse who feels annoyed when the patient's bell goes again cannot be said to care about the patient at that moment, but when she goes to help she is still caring for the patient. That is, she is not emotionally invested in the patient but she is tending the patient, and thus caring for her. If she does it well then her action has greater moral value than if, in her fatigued state, she makes a mistake. However, care cannot depend on being successful in order to count as care because we are sometimes mistaken about what is in the person's best interests and we are also susceptible to factors beyond our control preventing success (Collins 2015: 74).

Very often we do care about the people we are caring for. These are the cases that most readily spring to mind when we think about care. However, conceptually and in practice they do not have to go together (Collins 2015: 56). It can even be better if the professional does not feel emotional when providing care. For example, the doctors and nurses who have to give a small child chemotherapy know that they will cause her pain and that the side-effects of the drugs will be severe, but they must do it to save her life and try not to convey any distress for the child's sake. Professional detachment is a skill practitioners develop over time and they are praised for achieving it. However, professional detachment must never become indifference or callousness. The same is true of surrogacy. A surrogate who takes a very dispassionate view of the pregnancy but meticulously does all she can to ensure its success counts as caring for the intended baby because her intention is to fulfil its interests in being carried to term and born healthy. People tend to condemn surrogates for not having maternal feelings towards the baby. They fail to grasp two important and related points about surrogates. The first is that they do not have maternal feelings because they do not see themselves as the baby's mother, which is a defining feature of surrogacy. She might very well have positive feelings about the intended baby but she does not have to. The second point is that her care for the intended baby is what she *does* to help it thrive. We should not disparage her for not having the right feelings, whatever those might be.

Components of Trust in the Caring Professions

In the caring professions the fact that patients or clients have to trust the professional is the starting point for extensive reflection on the professional requirement to be trustworthy. When we say that patients have to trust, we mean that they have no alternative. The professions provide services that people cannot provide for themselves. The need often arises without the individual making a deliberate choice to avail herself of the services. Particularly in healthcare, need may also render the person unusually vulnerable and helpless.

Professional Obligations

What makes a professional trustworthy? When people seek medical help and become patients, for example, what makes it safe for them to give their trust? The patient is usually trusting a stranger when she seeks professional assistance. We have seen how perilous it can be to trust strangers, yet patients have to put their very lives in the hands of strangers. However, the dangers of trusting strangers we outlined earlier are substantially reduced by the professional's implicit promise to carry out the duties that come with her role (Koehn 1996: 198–199). In being accepted as a registered member of a profession, a person has made a commitment to act in accordance with the relevant law, regulations and codes of ethics. This commitment is likely to be made explicit in the form of information the patient is given about her rights. That pledge is a minimum requirement for trustworthiness.

A trustworthy professional has also committed to doing the job well and has done so for reasons to do with the job itself (Mullin 2005: 320). These reasons include such things as professional ideals or belief in the value of the work. The nursing literature, for example, explicitly calls for practitioners to develop a range of personal qualities including 'generosity, charity, [and] compassion' in order to be genuinely trustworthy (Dinç and Gastmans 2012: 231).

While commitment and values are very important to general trustworthiness, patients arrive with widely varying backgrounds, culture, past experiences and expectations. These individual differences affect how willing or able a person is to trust the people caring for them. Those practitioners must actively seek to gain the trust of that particular patient. Trustworthiness is a response to vulnerability and it has to be a response to the patient's actual vulnerability (Barnard 2016: 288).

Professional obligations go beyond what can be specified in a contract. Going to a doctor is not like calling a plumber. There is an enormous amount of uncertainty in addition to the risks that can be quantified. The professional makes an open-ended commitment to serve the patient's interests based on a promise and a belief in the importance of the work. They undertake to do the job well by responding to the individual needs of their patient and they realize that doing the job badly would have devastating results. They recognize the uniquely vulnerable state of the person for whom they care. These features of professional obligations apply also to surrogacy. The intended parents have individual histories of how they have arrived at the vulnerable state of needing to trust a stranger to carry a baby for them, which for same-sex couples can include a history of discrimination and negative stereotypes about them as potential parents. If the surrogate does not do her job well the results will indeed be devastating. However, as in medical care, failure is a possibility. Just as in medical care when nothing further can be done to assist the patient, if the surrogate acts with compassion, generosity and trustworthiness, the failure need not be as catastrophic to the wellbeing of the intended parents as it would be if it resulted from, or was accompanied by, a lack of the required ethical qualities.

Professional Vulnerability

Vulnerability is not one-sided. Professionals, especially those in the caring professions, are also vulnerable. No one is exempt from the physical and psychological vulnerabilities that come from being human. The patient may be vulnerable in a particular way and at a particular level but the doctor is a human being with limitations as well. Patients can exacerbate the doctor's vulnerability by their unreasonable behaviour or expectations. Some professional vulnerability arises out of their role and patients should be aware of it and respect it. Daryl Koehn (1996) thinks that they should have reasonable expectations, be 'self-critical' and understand that the professional might not always meet their expectations. One reason for this is that the professional cannot know for certain what those expectations are because they cannot be fully specified (Koehn 1996: 189). That is a direct consequence of the inevitable uncertainties in any complex setting. When she agrees to help, she is vulnerable in at least this one respect as a result. She therefore has to trust the patient to be reasonable. There is mutual trust in the relationship (Dinç and Gastmans 2012: 224). Similarly, the intended parents should recognize the surrogate's vulnerability, both as a person and as a surrogate. It is just as important that she can trust them as that they can trust her.

Power and the Professions

The professions are structured around protections for the clients because professional/client relationships are power-differentiated. The client is the weaker party with greater vulnerability to professionals acting opportunistically. We have been treating the professional and surrogate as analogous to each other and it may look as if we have things the wrong way round. The surrogate is usually the less powerful party to the arrangement. The point about analogies is that they show similarities but are not identical in every respect. The surrogate is analogous to the professional in many respects and the intended parents are vulnerable in ways analogous to patients. However, professionals derive their power from expertise that only they have. Their patients or clients are vulnerable because they are not in a position to evaluate whether they are receiving the right help or not. They lack the relevant expertise. Here our analogy breaks down. The intended parents are vulnerable not because the surrogate has expertise, though she certainly has to have skill, but because she has complete control over the gestation of their baby. That is a significant form of power but it is different from professional power. However, like professionals the surrogate is vulnerable to the intended parents' unreasonable behaviour. The intended parents can also renege on the agreement, which gives them a significant form of power. The professions are structured to protect members from that sort of behaviour. In the same way the professional model of surrogacy protects surrogates, as we show in Chap. 6.

The professional structure provides clearly defined constraints on what clients can expect and what they should not expect. It provides protection from the consequences of trusting a stranger. It puts a check on unreasonable demands by the client and allows for sanctions on the trustee should she act opportunistically. Regulating surrogacy along professional lines would make these protections available to intended parents and surrogates.

We now turn to exactly what it is the intended parents trust the surrogate to do, which is to provide care to the intended baby.

Gestational Care and Trust

Gestational care is unique in that the surrogate is the only person who can provide it. What the surrogate does or fails to do can make a significant difference to the outcome of the pregnancy even though many things that go wrong are beyond anyone's control. The intended baby's interests are fairly fundamental. The most important one is to be born healthy. Ideally the baby will be full term and normal weight. Others include not being at elevated risk for metabolic syndrome, to which the surrogate's weight and diet make a difference. Neonates depend on their mother's immunities to protect them from serious illnesses, such as whooping cough, until they are old enough to be immunized. The surrogate would need to give careful consideration to having vaccinations against that and possibly influenza, when she might not otherwise have done so. For interests like these it is tempting to say that all the surrogate needs to do is follow instructions about diet, exercise, immunizations and exposure to toxins in the environment. Where is the skill in that? However, that is not how pregnancy works. There are many situations, some serious, some less so, in which a decision has to be made that calls for good judgement, evaluation of numerous relevant facts and where there is no obviously right answer. The surrogate has the right to determine what happens to her body but she has also accepted obligations to the intended baby whose interests only she can serve.

Annette Baier (1986: 240) captures the nature of trust in this setting. 'Trust', she says, 'is letting other persons…take care of something the truster (sic) cares about, where such "caring for" involves some exercise of discretionary powers.' The intended parents who are unable to form a family without the surrogate's assistance, entrust her with their most cherished hopes and also their most fragile means to realizing those hopes. Even to reach the stage of having an embryo to implant they, and the surrogate, have endured an emotionally gruelling process. For the surrogate, and sometimes the intended mother, it will also have been a physically demanding one. Establishing a viable (as opposed to a chemical) pregnancy is again a time of immense anxiety and stress. Then the intended parents face all the risks of a pregnancy with the added measure of no control over the gestation.

Although surrogates sometimes joke about being the oven baking someone else's bread (Gelmann 2010), they are aware of the intended baby's interests and acutely aware of the risks to it while *in utero*. Some surrogates feel even more anxious about the welfare of the intended baby than they did about their own children at that stage. They do not feel a maternal bond to the intended baby but often do feel an emotional attachment where they care *about* the intended baby but do not feel that the baby is theirs. That cannot be too strongly emphasized as there appears to be considerable resistance among professionals, policy makers and the general public to the idea that the bond is not the 'natural' maternal one. Without grasping that, people will not be able to understand the nature of the care that surrogates give to the intended baby. It is not done for themselves, but for the intended baby itself and the intended parents. It is equally important to realize that, on the whole, surrogates see the intended baby's interests as independent of those of the intended parents.

People rightly suspect that to speak of care work is to speak of something that is highly gendered and consequently undervalued. It is a fact that women do most of the care work, whether that is of children, elders and other family members or professionally. It is also true that it tends to be low paid and seen as less valuable than other sorts of work. However, these are injustices rather than necessary conditions. We suspect that the willingness of society to tolerate or idealize altruistic surrogacy is a result of deeply entrenched sexism and hope that by showing how skilled and valuable the work of surrogates actually is we will contribute to removing some of that prejudice. It is true that only women can be surrogates but we would like to see reforms that raise their status rather than attempts to rationalize their unjust treatment. The professional model is predicated on their work being of high, not low, value.

Where does that leave the Allbrights and Candace? In order to facilitate mutual trust the selection of surrogates has to include the personal qualities that reduce the risk of opportunism. However, personal qualities are not enough by themselves to ensure a good relationship. The regulatory and legal framework has to foster trustworthy behaviour and include enforceable safeguards in the agreement that establishes the relationship. Safeguards should protect both intended parents and surrogates from the risks they are most likely to encounter. The inevitable uncertainties have to be carefully managed and, for that to happen, professional support has to be available at all times. In Chap. 6 we set out the process that intended parents and potential surrogates would follow.

Conclusion

Trust is central to successful surrogacy. The intended parents trust the surrogate to do what she has promised and the surrogate also trusts them to keep their promises to her. Trust is usually given by intended parents to a surrogate about whom they know little. We identified two forms of trust that are at work in these decisions: calculative and relational trust. The conditions that increase trustworthiness differ according to the nature of the trust that dominates. A good contract works best for calculative trust, which dominates business transactions, as it sets up the relationship in such a way that it is in the interests of the trustee to fulfil it. Risks can be quantified and factored in. Relational trust, which is everyday trust, relies on a prior history of interaction and a range of cues. Mistakes about whom to trust occur when the parties use the wrong sort of mechanism or select the wrong cues. Uncertainty, which cannot be quantified, is the main difficulty in relational trust because the intentions and beliefs of the trustee are inaccessible to others. All decisions to trust involve both calculative and relational factors.

The intended parents can make mistakes by focussing on easy to process, but irrelevant personal cues to evaluate the trustworthiness of the surrogate. Surrogates in turn often base their trust on what they hope for rather than what the cues actually indicate is likely. Such mistakes can lead to misunderstanding and disappointment. Further, there is a significant power imbalance in surrogacy, especially transnational surrogacy. Power and status affect trust because the high-power individual is likely to be less aware of the interests of the low-power trustee. Status can mitigate the effects of power because status depends on how others perceive the individual. The social distance between intended parents and surrogates makes it more likely that surrogates' needs will not be met.

The caring professions are structured to increase the trustworthiness of practitioners and also to protect them from unreasonable demands or mistreatment by clients. Registration is an indication to clients that the practitioner has made a commitment to behave ethically and has achieved a satisfactory standard of expertise. There are sanctions for breaches of standards, including deregistration. Professional trust minimizes the risks associated with trusting a stranger. It recognizes the vulnerabilities of both client and practitioner. We argued that these features should be adapted for the regulation of surrogacy.

Surrogacy relationships are more likely to be successful if they use the same structure for building trust that the caring professions use. These provide for both types of trust because both types are always present in complex relationships involving open-ended commitments that cannot be fully specified in advance. Professional trust requires a supportive legal and regulatory framework and that means surrogacy requires something very similar. We now set out the framework necessary for the professional model.

References

Baier, A. (1986). Trust and antitrust. *Ethics, 96*(2), 231–260.

Barnard, D. (2016). Vulnerability and trustworthiness. *Cambridge Quarterly of Healthcare Ethics, 25*(02), 288–300.

Bicchieri, C., Xiao, E., & Muldoon, R. (2011). Trustworthiness is a social norm, but trusting is not. *Politics, Philosophy & Economics, 10*(2), 170–187.

Braynov, S. (2013). What human trust is and is not: On the biology of human trust. *2013 AAAI Spring Symposium Series*, 10–15.

Collins, S. (2015). *The core of care ethics*. New York: Palgrave Macmillan.

Dinç, L., & Gastmans, C. (2012). Trust and trustworthiness in nursing: An argument-based literature review. *Nursing Inquiry, 19*(3), 223–237.

Dunning, D., Anderson, J. E., Schlösser, T., et al. (2014). Trust at zero acquaintance: More a matter of respect than expectation of reward. *Journal of Personality and Social Psychology, 107*(1), 122–141.

Evans, A. M., & Krueger, J. I. (2016). Bounded prospection in dilemmas of trust and reciprocity. *Review of General Psychology, 20*(1), 17–28.

Gargiulo, M., & Ertug, G. (2006). The dark side of trust. In R. Bachmann & A. Zaheer (Eds.), *Handbook of trust research* (pp. 165–186). Northampton, MA: Edward Elgar.

Gelmann, E. (2010). I'm just the oven, it's totally their bun: The power and necessity of the Federal Government to regulate commercial gestational surrogacy arrangements and protect the legal rights of intended parents. *Women's Rights Law Reporter, 32,* 159–192.

Goel, S., Bell, G. G., & Pierce, J. L. (2005). The perils of Pollyanna: Development of the over-trust construct. *Journal of Business Ethics, 58*(1), 203–218.

James, H. S., Jr. (2014). You can have your trust and calculativeness, too: Uncertainty, trustworthiness and the Williamson thesis. *Journal of Trust Research, 4*(1), 57–65.

Koehn, D. (1996). Should we trust in trust? *American Business Law Journal, 34*(2), 183–204.

Lammers, J., Galinsky, A. D., Gordijn, E. H., & Otten, S. (2012). Power increases social distance. *Social Psychological and Personality Science, 3*(3), 282–290.

Lount, R. B., Jr., & Pettit, N. C. (2012). The social context of trust: The role of status. *Organizational Behavior and Human Decision Processes, 117*(1), 15–23.

Lumineau, F. (2014). How contracts influence trust and distrust. *Journal of Management, 43*(5), 1553-1577.

Magee, J. C., & Galinsky, A. D. (2008). Social hierarchy: The self-reinforcing nature of power and status. *Academy of Management Annals, 2*(1), 351–398.

Margalit, Y. (2014). In defense of surrogacy agreements: A modern contract law perspective. *William & Mary Journal of Women and the Law, 20*(2), 423–468.

Mullin, A. (2005). Trust, social norms, and motherhood. *Journal of Social Philosophy, 36*(3), 316–330.

Pande, A. (2014). *Wombs in labor: Transnational commercial surrogacy in India.* New York: Columbia University Press.

Poppo, L., Zhou, K. Z., & Li, J. J. (2016). When can you trust "trust"? Calculative trust, relational trust, and supplier performance. *Strategic Management Journal, 37*(4), 724–741.

Rousseau, D. M., Sitkin, S. B., Burt, R. S., & Camerer, C. (1998). Introduction to special topic forum: Not so different after all: A cross-discipline view of trust. *The Academy of Management Review, 23*(3), 393–404.

Schilke, O., & Cook, K. S. (2015). Sources of alliance partner trustworthiness: Integrating calculative and relational perspectives. *Strategic Management Journal, 36*(2), 276–297.

Schilke, O., Reimann, M., & Cook, K. S. (2015). Power decreases trust in social exchange. *Proceedings of the National Academy of Sciences of the United States of America, 112*(42), 12950–12955.

Skinner, D., Dietz, G., & Weibel, A. (2014). The dark side of trust: When trust becomes a 'poisoned chalice'. *Organization, 21*(2), 206–224.

Smith, P. K., & Magee, J. C. (2015). The interpersonal nature of power and status. *Current Opinion in Behavioral Sciences, 3,* 152–156.

Stevens, L. E., & Fiske, S. T. (2000). Motivated impressions of a powerholder: Accuracy under task dependency and misperception under evaluation dependency. *Personality and Social Psychology Bulletin, 26*(8), 907–922.

Sturm, R. E., & Antonakis, J. (2015). Interpersonal power: A review, critique, and research agenda. *Journal of Management, 41*(1), 136–163.

Thielmann, I., & Hilbig, B. E. (2015). Trust: An integrative review from a person–situation perspective. *Review of General Psychology, 19*(3), 249–277.

Vanneste, B. S., Puranam, P., & Kretschmer, T. (2014). Trust over time in exchange relationships: Meta-analysis and theory. *Strategic Management Journal, 35*(12), 1891–1902.

Weber, J. M., Malhotra, D., & Murnighan, J. K. (2005). Normal acts of irrational trust: Motivated attributions and the trust development process. *Revisiting the Meaning of Leadership, 75*–101.

Williamson, O. E. (1993). Calculativeness, trust, and economic organization. *The Journal of Law & Economics, 36*(1), 453–486.

Zahra, S. A., Yavuz, R. I., & Ucbasaran, D. (2006). How much do you trust me? The dark side of relational trust in new business creation in established companies. *Entrepreneurship: Theory & Practice* 30(4): 541–559.

5

Law and Regulation

Introduction

There have been many serious attempts to produce legal and regulatory frameworks that bring order to the practice of surrogacy. Israel has a widely admired system and several states in the US have tried to adopt legislation that is permissive and clear about the parties' rights and responsibilities. The difficulty is to develop coherent, principled law and policy. The first problem is that all legislation is a response to something that has happened and designed to remedy just that aspect of surrogacy. The second is that the dominant models of surrogacy (altruistic and commercial) are flawed, so that legislating in favour of, or against, either model spreads flawed thinking through the regulatory system. The third is that empirical evidence about the actual effects of surrogacy is either ignored or misunderstood so that rules protect parties from the wrong set of dangers and expose them to different ones. We think that the lack of a coherent, principled, and evidence-based approach to surrogacy undermines most current recommendations for legal and regulatory reform, however well intentioned. For that reason we approach the process differently.

© The Author(s) 2017
R. Walker and L. van Zyl, *Towards a Professional Model of Surrogate Motherhood*,
DOI 10.1057/978-1-137-58658-2_5

We begin by considering the main objective of surrogacy, which is to enable people who cannot bring a pregnancy to term to become legal parents. To meet this objective there must be a mechanism by which their legal parentage of the resulting offspring is assured. Further, specific provisions have to be made to protect the rights of the woman who gestates the intended baby/babies and to uphold the human rights of children. We apply the professional model to these issues and then work our way back to the legal and regulatory framework that needs to be in place to support it. We begin with the question of parentage.

Legal Parentage

The test of parentage has to work for all types of surrogacy relationship from traditional, where the surrogate is the genetic mother and (one of) the intended father(s) is the genetic father, to standard gestational, where the surrogate is not the genetic mother but one or both of the intended parents are the genetic parents, to the growing phenomenon of gestational surrogacy with donor gametes where none of the parties is genetically related to the babies.

Regulation needs to address three aspects of parentage: its basis, mechanism and timing. The basis for legal parentage in family law varies widely but there are four criteria that can be treated separately. The principal grounds for parentage are genetic relationship, gestation, best interests and intention. From the perspective of surrogacy, the former two are an unhelpful inheritance. They have a long history in the courts when parental rights and responsibilities are being assigned, and generally serve the best interests of the child. However, in the context of surrogacy they are very problematic. We begin by considering the suitability of a genetic relationship as the grounds for parentage.

Genetic Relationship

Currently, the main reason for using genetic relationship in parental disputes is to determine paternity, and thus who has parental rights and responsibilities. In surrogacy, by contrast, there is no consistent genetic relationship to rely on. In this sense, surrogacy is similar to donor-assisted reproduction, where either or both of the intended parents are genetically unrelated to the baby. In traditional surrogacy, at least the surrogate and possibly also the intended father will be genetically related to the baby. On the other end of the spectrum, in gestational surrogacy, it is possible for neither the surrogate nor the intended parents to be genetically related to the baby.

In donor-assisted reproduction, a genetic relationship is not a criterion for legal parentage. We think the same ought to be the case in traditional surrogacy: the genetic relationship has to be disregarded if the purpose of the arrangement is to be achieved. This would also end discrimination against couples who are doubly infertile, recognize the parental status of unrelated partners in non-traditional families, including same-sex couples, and put everyone on an equal footing.

There is a second problem with giving weight to genetic relationships that actually undermines the claim that genetic relationship is important. In both the UK and New Zealand, for example, at least one of the intended parents is required to provide the gametes. When the baby is born, however, the genetic relationship is considered to be irrelevant to parental status. Instead, the surrogate and her partner are the legal parents. That means the child could be completely unrelated to its legal parents, while its genetic parent(s) could be denied legal parentage if the surrogate refuses to relinquish the child or the court refuses to transfer parental rights. It appears, then, that the genetic relationship only matters when the courts and policy makers say it does. The outcomes can be perverse.

Those jurisdictions where gametes are demanded from an intended parent as a condition of approving the surrogacy arrangement are doing something profoundly unethical. They are effectively treating the intended parents as gamete donors. Gamete donors give unconditionally. While the donating intended parent can be said to consent to the use of his or her gametes to establish a pregnancy in the surrogate, the scope of that consent is strictly limited. Intended parents who supply gametes consent to their use to produce a child for themselves. They are not donors who provide gametes for others to form their families, yet that is effectively what they are obliged to be. They have no legal right to the resulting offspring and no way to protect themselves from serious emotional harm. Their gametes are potentially used for a purpose that they did not, and would not, consent to.

Gestation

Another important criterion for determining parentage is gestation. It is only in recent history that gestation and maternity could be separated. The principle that the mother is always certain has been the bedrock for maternal rights (Bainham 2008). Gestation as a determinant of motherhood is seen as intuitively obvious and not in need of justification. Surrogacy, however, provides a serious challenge to this assumption because the woman gestating the intended baby is not the baby's mother as far as she and the intended parents are concerned, regardless of whether she is also the genetic mother. Suddenly, the question of why and how gestation establishes motherhood needs an answer.

Anca Gheaus (2012) provides a detailed account of how gestation grounds parental rights. It is probably the best recent treatment of the issue, reflecting contemporary concerns. We give it serious scrutiny because the reasoning behind it appears to be what motivates the use of gestation in the courts and public understanding. However, we conclude that it is unsuccessful. Gheaus's argument is that the costs of pregnancy and the bond that forms between the pregnant woman and the fetus are the basis of the woman's right to parent that baby. Genetic relationships are irrelevant and the gestational mother's right to parent turns out to be close to inalienable. We have four areas of concern that we will examine in turn. The first is that the account is at best only weakly supportive of parental rights and that surrogacy provides a counter example to its claims. Second, Gheaus subscribes to what we call the 'helpless vessel' view of pregnant women that undermines their autonomy and rationality. Third, the empirical evidence she cites in support of her argument is deeply flawed. Robust empirical research in psychology contradicts her. Fourth, her argument to ground the non-gestating parent's rights also supports the parental rights of intended parents.

Physical Investment

Gheaus argues that certain facts about gestation establish the moral right of the gestational mother to parent the baby. It is uncontroversial to say that the investment of the gestational mother is greater than that of her 'supportive partner' because only she can provide the bodily resources the fetus needs to grow and develop. However, over and above those resources, the gestating mother is 'typically highly emotionally invested in the pregnancy' and her relationship with the fetus is 'to some extent unavoidable' (Gheaus 2012: 436). Gheaus goes on to say that 'many—perhaps most—expectant parents form a poignantly embodied, but also emotional, intimate relationship with their fetus.' (Gheaus 2012: 446) Although Gheaus uses this to bolster her argument for the gestational mother's parental rights, it also shows that a gestating mother can avoid forming a close emotional bond with the fetus.

Surrogacy provides precisely the atypical circumstances in which the relevant bond does not form because the surrogate does not invest emotionally the way parents do when they expect to be raising the child. As the relationship and bond formation are avoidable, we argue that gestation cannot form the basis of parental rights, especially given the intentions of the surrogate herself. The assumptions Gheaus makes about the effect of pregnancy on women suggests that she does not give the surrogate's intentions much weight.

Emotional and Social Costs

In addition to the physical costs of pregnancy there are emotional and social costs, such as fear of miscarriage and 'patronising and uninvited familiarity' (Gheaus 2012: 447). She argues that the supportive partners play an important role in this regard:

> [They are] the main source of emotional, practical and financial support of their pregnant partner: they can accompany her on medical visits and support her during childbirth, share and try to soothe her worries, relieve her of some of her regular work and serve as an often-needed interface

between her the insufficiently accommodating outer world (Gheaus 2012: 448).

This description depicts the pregnant woman as extraordinarily fragile and the partner as protector rather than supporter. It is at odds with the models of empowerment that women in the developed world now take for granted. Typically, pregnant woman experience some but not all of the physical symptoms of pregnancy. Usually these are mild rather than severe. Thanks to legal and social changes that make continuing to work during pregnancy normal rather than exceptional, women need not be financially dependent on their partners. Indeed, surrogates are paid to be pregnant and have even less need of the supportive partner's money. They tend not to need a shield between themselves and the irritating—but usually well meaning—members of the public. More importantly, normal pregnancies give rise to fewer worries and anxieties than at any time in human history. Women do not generally fear for their lives or those of their babies when they give birth. They are far more in control of the way their pregnancies and labour are managed than ever before so they keep their autonomy. Nothing can be done to a pregnant woman without her consent unless it is an emergency and she has lost the capacity to give it. Where women's right to autonomy is not respected, it is an injustice rather than an inevitable part of the burden of pregnancy. And there are benefits to pregnancy, which Gheaus has to concede, though she claims that '...the benefits and joys of pregnancy do not cancel out the costs, and do not turn pregnancy into an intrinsically desirable experience.' (Gheaus 2012: 448) She offers no supporting evidence for this claim and it denies the validity of claims by some surrogates (not to mention other women) that they enjoy being pregnant (Jacobson 2016).

Surrogates are as much helpless vessels as other women in Gheaus's world. She says: 'Is it possible to wave (sic) one's right to keep one's birth baby before one knows exactly what burdens the pregnancy will entail, and what kind of relationship one will establish with the newborn?' (Gheaus 2012: 454) The implied answer is 'no.' In a more recent article specifically about surrogacy she makes it clear that the answer is no. '[S]urrogates, too, may undergo—albeit involuntarily, and possibly unconsciously—some anticipation, hoping and projection.' (Gheaus 2016: 26) These are characteristic of pregnancy, and surrogacy can be no exception because that is what gestation does to women.

Maternal-Fetal-Attachment

According to Gheaus, a relationship forms between the gestating mother and the fetus that cements the parental rights of the gestating mother. In her view the relationship is mutual and should be preserved because it is in the baby's interest. The moral right to parent her biological baby cannot be transferred because of the newborn's attachment to her, which began in the womb. She concludes that surrogacy contracts should always be void (Gheaus 2016: 21).

The empirical argument Gheaus puts forward is based on the reality of this relationship. However, the idea of maternal-fetal-attachment (MFA) or, as it is sometimes called, maternal-fetal-relationship (MFR), is flawed for two main reasons. The first is that researchers do not keep two different processes separate. They do not treat birth as the completion of one stage of development and the beginning of an entirely new one in which the infant starts to interact with the people around it for the first time. It takes the rigorous concept of infant attachment and backdates the beginning of that process to the antenatal period. But whatever it is that researchers are measuring during pregnancy, it is not attachment.

Infant attachment to its primary caregiver is a mutual relationship that develops over the course of the first year of life. It continues to change beyond that period. The infant engages in behaviour designed to trigger the 'caregiving system' in the person looking after it (Walsh 2010: 449). It does not have to be the mother but in this context we are talking about the mother. During pregnancy the woman can engage her caregiving system by thinking of herself as a mother and imagining herself as a caregiver. This is an entirely different process to infant attachment because the fetus is not doing anything. It is all coming from the woman herself. In fact, her thoughts and feelings during pregnancy do not predict how well or badly the baby will attach to her (Walsh 2010:

450). There are many other variables that influence the success or failure of infant attachment. Walsh holds that it is best to think of the time during pregnancy as 'prenatal caregiving'. Attachment does not begin before birth.

It is just as misleading to refer to a relationship between the fetus and gestating mother. A relationship involves interactions between two parties and during pregnancy the fetus and gestating mother are not interacting. It goes only one way, consisting of the thoughts and feelings of the mother about the fetus as it develops. So, it is neither attachment nor relational. They do not embark on a relationship until after birth (Redshaw and Martin 2013).

The second problem is to do with the research into MFA itself. It is weak because it relies solely on self-report by pregnant women who answer questionnaires about their attitudes. Infant attachment research uses both self-report on questionnaires and observation. The researchers can watch how infants and mothers interact. Mothers can quite genuinely believe that their babies are more securely attached than they are or they could feel that they have to respond to surveys in the 'correct' way so that they do not appear to be 'bad' mothers. There are socially approved attitudes to motherhood and babies that women often feel they have to express. This is an example of 'social desirability bias' (Porter 2015).

Because there are also socially approved attitudes to pregnancy, the social desirability bias is likely to arise in MFA research. There are no interactions to observe so attitudes are all that can be measured. Women will report having the attitudes towards the fetus that are socially expected of them. That is what happened in a study of MFA conducted by Ellen Lorenceau et al. (2015). The researchers compared the MFA of surrogates to that of women who were pregnant with their own babies. Both groups reported the same levels of attachment, which suggests that surrogates do form a maternal bond with the intended baby and feel the same way about it as they would their own babies. However, such a finding is at odds with evidence from interview-based research with surrogates that shows no maternal bond with the fetus. The questionnaire used in the Lorenceau study included a social desirability scale designed to detect whether respondents were answering honestly about how they felt or were giving answers that showed them in a positive light, that is, as having the attitudes society expects women to have towards the developing fetus. A high score would indicate the presence of social desirability bias. The surrogates did indeed score highly on this scale, from which we should conclude that they reported having socially approved attitudes rather than the ones they actually had.

Some researchers think that MFA is unambiguously good and that where it is low the aim should be to increase it. In other words, not only is there a socially approved attitude to the fetus, it is also widely believed that women who do not feel a bond should be helped to develop one. Against this, Judi Walsh et al. (2013) argue that there are circumstances in which a degree of detachment is healthy, such as when the pregnancy is high risk. A wider concern is that the promotion of MFA sends a message that there is a 'Right Way' to be a mother. If you do not have a strong bond with your developing baby then you are not a good mother. Making women feel guilty or inadequate is not desirable (Walsh et al. 2013: 496). Surrogacy is another case where the healthy attitude towards the fetus is one of detachment. We find the focus on MFA disturbing because it is likely to increase the stigma that surrogates already face. It signals to them that they are not normal because they do not have the 'right' maternal feelings. As MFA has no effect on fetal development and does not influence infant attachment, its prominence is potentially harmful.

Non-gestational Parenthood

The gestating mother cannot be the only one with parental rights. Gheaus's explanation of how the non-gestating parent acquires rights further undermines the gestation criterion. She argues that supportive partners gain parental rights by sharing some of the costs of pregnancy and providing the support detailed above. The point is further emphasized when she states that they are

> capable of being direct participants in the process of creating a relationship with the baby during pregnancy. With the help of medical technology

they can see the fetus and hear its heartbeat as early as the bearing mother; during the last stages of pregnancy they can feel the baby, talk to it and be heard by it. Just like the mother, they can experience the fears, hopes and fantasies triggered by the growing fetus (Gheaus 2012: 450).

If we substitute 'intended parents' for 'supportive partner' it is clear that they too can acquire parental rights. One possible objection to such a substitution is that there is something about the relationship between the gestating mother and her supportive partner that qualifies him or her as a parent but would not qualify intended parents in the case of surrogacy. Gheaus does not make that move. In fact, she goes on to describe how 'adoptive parents' could form the same relationship as supportive partners prior to the baby's birth (Gheaus 2012: 453). This is a precise description of what intended parents do. Either Gheaus has to admit that the gestating mother is the only, or principal, real parent or she has to allow that social parents, including intended parents, can acquire equal parental rights through the process available to supportive partners.

Lindsey Porter (2015: 14) argues that surrogate pregnancies are less costly, both emotionally and economically, than other pregnancies, and that many of these costs can be compensated. Gheaus's admission that it is possible to avoid forming a maternal bond with the intended baby, together with the fact that it is possible to meet many of the costs of pregnancy, can be used to argue in support of paid surrogacy. But what if the surrogate does form a bond with the fetus? Porter's response is that '[f]eeling attached to something cannot generate a right to that something.' (Porter 2015: 23) As there is no evidence of any effect of the gestational mother's feelings on the fetus, we think they are irrelevant to the question of parental rights unless the claim of parental rights is a form of ownership (which is most emphatically not what Gheaus or other scholars intend).

Best Interests

Close examination of the gestation claim shows that it is not a sound basis for adjudicating parental status in surrogacy but it remains an influential component of policy and legal decision-making. It appears that it is difficult for theorists to let go of the notion that what happens emotionally and biologically in pregnancy is relevant to the baby's interests. Although the empirical literature to which we now turn shows that this view is mistaken, courts often take it into account when determining the best interests of the child. However, they could be making decisions that are contrary to the child's best interests.

The literature on attachment shows that a putative gestational bond is of no developmental importance to the fetus. The uterine environment itself has a significant influence on development so what the mother does is important. How she feels about the fetus is not. Infants attach to their caregivers regardless of whether the caregiver also gestated them. The caregiver is a 'safe haven' who provides a 'secure base' from which to explore the world (Van der Voort et al. 2014: 165). The infant will form a secure attachment to the person who fulfils that role. If no one does then attachment will be insecure or disordered. The gestational mother has no advantage in this regard.

One of the myths about attachment is that there is a sensitive or critical period in which an infant or newborn bonds with its mother and that if this does not happen, or the bond is disrupted, the rest of the child's life will be negatively affected. Adoption studies contradict this popular belief: 'Children who were adopted before 12 months of age showed secure attachments as often as non-adopted children' (Van den Dries et al. 2009: 416). Even infants who have been maltreated prior to adoption can form secure attachments to their new caregivers (Altenhofen et al. 2013; Van den Dries et al. 2009). Attachment should be viewed as a process that occurs over the course of an individual's development, with less weight given to its status in the first year of life when the capacity for secure attachment is at its most malleable. This may be counterintuitive, even countercultural, but no weight should be given to the 'bond' with its gestational mother. Nor should the person who has the baby for the first few months necessarily be given custody based simply on an attachment. The child's primary interest is in having parents who are sensitive to its needs.

Parental sensitivity is the best predictor of secure attachment. If the parent or other primary caregiver is not sensitive and responsive to the child's needs during their interactions the child is less likely to be securely attached. Parental sensitivity varies in influence as the child develops. During adolescence it is less influential, perhaps because that is when individuals begin to choose their own environments and when peer relationships are more significant, but the change in adolescent attachment may be temporary (Schoenmaker et al. 2015). Parental sensitivity itself is not always stable due to changes in the environment for parents, such as 'divorce, unemployment [and] poverty' (Schoenmaker et al. 2015: 242). These can have a negative effect but there can also be environmental changes that improve parental sensitivity and attachment.

Experiences of attachment over childhood and adolescence lead to the development of an individual's 'internal working model' of attachment that provides their style and guides their expectations of others. They carry this style into their own parenting (Van der Voort et al. 2014: 167). If the gestational mother's internal working model reflects her own negative experiences of attachment then the chances of the infant attaching securely to her are lower. The quality of attachment and its influence, then, can vary over the course of a childhood for a host of environmental reasons (Schoenmaker et al. 2015). Attachment is not a moment and is not confined to one particular caregiver. Nor does the caregiver have to stand in a specific relationship to the child prior to becoming the primary caregiver.

Sometimes a surrogate claims that it would be in the child's best interests to be raised by her because she would make a better parent than the intended parents. We take the principle of best interests seriously and think it clearly relevant to some important aspects of surrogacy, transnational surrogacy in particular, when the child's rights can be in jeopardy because of national laws regarding citizenship. However, when choosing between competing claims for parentage of a child from a surrogacy relationship, it is not clear that it is possible to be confident about what is in the child's best interests.

The child has a strong interest in having parents who will be adequate or better over the entire course of its development to adulthood. But children are not passive recipients of parenting. The characteristics children have can elicit different parenting responses and these can play a significant role in determining the type of parenting they receive. The studies in this area look at differential parenting within families, that is, where siblings evoke different parental responses even where they are all genetically related. The child's characteristics can be caused by genetic, uterine or environmental factors, including gene-environment interactions (Jenkins et al. 2016). A boy who exhibits 'externalizing behavior' will evoke different responses from the same parents than a girl, or a boy who does not have problem behaviour. The age of the child is similarly important. That is not to say that differential parenting is necessarily wrong, although it certainly can put a child at risk in a number of ways, but it does point to a significant variable that is often overlooked. In advance of knowing what sort of child it is, it is difficult to assess how the candidate parents would parent it. Parents' own personalities and experiences of adversity influence their parenting as well. Marital conflict is also a risk factor (Jenkins et al. 2016: 58). In surrogacy disputes, unlike other custody disputes that arise through marital breakdown, marital conflict is usually an unknown variable that cannot be predicted. A happy couple does not necessarily stay happy. Given the complexity of the influences on parenting, we think that a best interests test to determine who will be the better parents is unlikely to be robust, except in the most glaringly obvious cases.

A further concern about the best interests principle is that it can be used to discriminate against non-traditional families, especially gay men, on the specious grounds that it is in the child's best interests to have a mother rather than two fathers. The claim that a child needs a mother and a father can be used against lesbian couples. We think that in surrogacy relationships, intention is the safest principle for determining parentage of the child.

Intention-Based Parentage

A useful definition of 'intended parent' has emerged from the US courts. An intended parent is 'one whose intent is to become the legal parent of a child born of assisted reproduction or surrogacy. To be an intended parent does not require that one have a genetic relationship to the child.' (Storrow 2015: 209) A consistent and coherent policy can be built around this definition. Intention to parent is the strongest ground for parentage in surrogacy because the arrangement literally only exists because the intended parents intend to parent the baby and the surrogate does not. The negative version of intention to parent is just as important as the positive one. The surrogate, in spite of gestational links and sometimes genetic ones, does not want to parent the baby. It should not be as difficult as it appears to be because the same assumption is built into assisted reproductive technology (ART) with donor gametes. Donors give on the condition that they do not intend to parent any resulting offspring. Their donation is also received on that condition. Desire to parent would be grounds for rejecting the donation, and threat of parental obligations would be enough to stop people from donating. They are explicitly protected from this risk, which can cause complications for intended parents. We think it should be a small step to accept that surrogates act on the same condition. Unfortunately, the fact of gestation tends to obscure this similarity with gamete donors.

Objections to Intention-Based Parentage

There are some important objections to the use of intention as the sole criterion for establishing legal parentage. The obvious point is that it appears to allow the intended parents to change their minds. They could, at any point, say that they no longer intend to parent the baby. If the surrogate also does not intend to parent then the baby has no parents or, if the surrogate feels she cannot abandon the child, which has happened in some cases, she is left with a baby to raise. The cost of parenting a child is high and the surrogate is likely to have fewer financial resources and support than the intended parents.

To avoid this problem the professional model requires the intended parents to accept parental responsibility from the time the agreement is entered into. The regulatory mechanisms we propose ensure that the surrogate is never left with the baby. If the intended parents choose not to parent the baby they are in the same situation as natural parents who choose to relinquish their child and the relevant statutory authorities step in to find parents for the baby according to their protocols. The surrogate might apply to adopt the baby if she really wants to, but she would be on the same footing as any other potential adoptive parent and has no obligation whatever to offer.

Intention makes a genetic relationship redundant because, whatever the genetic status of the parties in relation to the intended baby, the intention to parent is found in the use of a surrogacy relationship in the first place. It is important to remember that most surrogacy relationships do not lead to disputes over parentage of the child. The surrogate holds to her intention not to parent and, where a transfer of parental rights is required, agrees to it readily. It is a formality, but one that can be time-consuming, stressful and costly.

There is a potential vulnerability: the surrogate's intention could change. The professional model does not permit the intended parents to change their minds after a pregnancy has been established and it cannot permit the surrogate to change hers either. This sits uncomfortably for many people who still intuitively think gestation creates a mother. Although the courts and the public readily assume that the reason she changes her mind is the bond she has formed with the baby and the powerful effect of gestation on her, we do not actually know that this is the case. Jenni Millbank (2015) suggests that relationships break down because of a lack of professional support. When this happens and the dispute ends in court, it is only to be expected that the parties will use whatever legal arguments are available to them in that jurisdiction. If claiming a bond would be successful then surrogates are likely to claim that they had a bond with the baby. We should not assume that it is the genuine reason behind the claim unless there is independent supporting evidence. If Millbank is correct then provision of support, such as that required in the professional model, would greatly reduce the risk of difficulty over relinquishment. Women likely to experience problems would not be registered. One of the consequences of exercising one's autonomy is that sometimes a decision is irrevocable. Surrogacy has to be one of those cases because a baby's future and that of its intended parents depend on that promise being kept. Even if she has developed a bond to the intended baby she cannot be allowed to act on it. The consequences for the baby and the intended parents are too severe.

Mechanisms and Timing

The 'when' and the 'how' of recognizing parentage are just as important as the 'what'. Current mechanisms involve the transfer of parental rights and responsibilities. In some jurisdictions these may be done prior to the birth of the baby but most occur after birth. However, all forms of transfer, regardless of their timing, are in effect forms of adoption. In all cases, the surrogate has some standing as a presumptive or legal mother that she can attempt to assert, or that the courts have to be persuaded that she does not possess. The intended baby's legal status will depend to a degree on when the jurisdiction recognizes it as a person. In New Zealand, for example, the baby is a person with rights from birth but not prior to birth—even during labour, the baby is not a person. Some states recognize the fetus as a rights bearing individual and can make pre-birth decisions for it.

A change to the timing of a parentage order does not eliminate the essential incoherence of the policy, which is that the baby is being transferred from the people who were never its parents to the people who were already its parents. A further difficulty is that a transfer involves some statutory scrutiny of the intended parents, the surrogate and the agreement and the longer this is delayed the more difficult it becomes. Bringing in social services after the baby is born to approve the intended parents as adoptive parents (in New Zealand) or, worse, up to 6 months after the baby has been placed in the intended parents' care (in the UK), is both too late and too uncertain. Social workers are almost never going to say no, but the intended parents worry that they will (Crawshaw et al. 2013). While judges making parental orders in the UK have a record of going to extreme lengths to justify granting the order, even when the intended parents are blatantly in breach of the law, they are not able to say this in advance, and this causes uncertainty for the parents. Reform is clearly needed to provide a principled basis to this process.

Our Proposal

We think that the problem lies with a transfer being involved at all. The surrogacy agreement should establish parentage and the intended parents' commitment to take the baby is binding from that point. In other words, a transfer does not take place. The surrogate does not relinquish the baby because it was never hers to begin with. If the adoption/transfer model is replaced with a properly regulated agreement as a means of establishing parentage it would have the following implications. Instead of transferring parental rights from one set of parents to another, the intended parents would be recognised as the legal parents from the moment the baby is born. Thus involvement of the courts would be unnecessary. All other statutory agencies would have finished their tasks considerably in advance of the baby's birth. This does not mean that nothing can be done if problems arise later but it does mean that all questions over the intended parents as parents would be treated the way they would be in any other pregnancy. If that means social services are waiting to remove the baby from their care (or prevent them taking charge of it), then it is no different to other care proceedings. These cases would be extremely rare and should not be given undue weight in the course of reforming surrogacy law.

Some scholars see the presumptive or actual parenthood of the surrogate as empowering for her and protection against exploitation (Margalit 2014). However, we argue that well-regulated surrogacy would provide all the protection she needs. The intended parents have significant obligations towards her and the framework we propose would ensure that these were met. The surrogate's rights might not include keeping the baby but they are far from trivial.

Surrogacy Agreements

The surrogacy agreements themselves would be in a standard form that had been approved for use by the regulatory authority. There would always be scope for accommodating legitimate preferences but these would be limited to clauses that are lawful and ethical and to which the surrogate had freely consented. Not only would standardized agreements protect the rights of the surrogate, they would also speed up the approval process for the intended parents and reduce the legal costs incurred in drawing them up. This would benefit all parties and reduce the incentive to choose riskier transnational surrogacy.

The surrogate has a right to fair compensation. Currently, commercial surrogacy makes payment part of the contractual negotiations and, where agencies are used, the intended parents have little say over how much of it goes to the surrogate herself. As we saw in Chap. 2, the situation is particularly disturbing in transnational surrogacy. Payment is often conditional on reaching certain stages of the pregnancy and on undergoing certain procedures, such as amniocentesis and Caesarean section, which means that there is a financial disincentive to refuse even when the surrogate is reluctant to undergo the procedure.

Under the professional model, fees would be set by the regulatory body that licenses clinics and registers surrogates. The fee paid to the surrogate would be independent of the fees paid to the clinic for treatment and could not be negotiated up or down. The surrogate retains all her rights as a pregnant woman. She is the patient of any health practitioners involved, which means she alone has the right to make decisions about the pregnancy and labour management (Chervenak and McCullough 2009). She has the right to confidentiality, which means that she cannot be required to disclose information to the intended parents and that health professionals would need her consent before they disclosed information. These basic rights could not (and cannot) be contracted away (Drabiak-Syed 2011). The intended parents simply have to accept these conditions as it would be unethical to permit anything else. No one can be expected to give up their basic rights. We do not underestimate the difficulty for them in doing so, which is why professional support for them and the surrogate throughout the process is such an integral part of the professional model.

The professionals who are involved at different stages, both prenatally and postnatally, need to be aware of the surrogate's role as patient and how it changes after the birth. This is why we recommend fully integrated health services so that there is seamless recognition of the intended parents as the parents from the moment the baby is born as well as continuity of care for the surrogate as she recovers from the birth. Surrogacy is not a common route to parenthood and it is sometimes difficult for midwives and staff in birthing centres to grasp that they should be dividing their normal practices between two parties. The intended parents are the ones whose introduction to parenthood begins with the newborn who is their responsibility alone. The surrogate is not the mother but she is a woman who has just given birth and requires postnatal care. Holistic care, the foundation of much modern obstetric practice, needs revising for surrogacy relationships to ensure that the different parties receive what they are entitled to.

To prevent exploitation and coercion, all surrogacy arrangements, including traditional, would be formal. All surrogates face the same risks and are equally deserving of protection from them. A friend or family member should go through the same process of registration as any other potential surrogate to ensure that she is medically and psychologically fit to undertake it and also that she is freely consenting. The registration process would be confidential so that she could be candid about whether she is under any pressure to do it. With an approved agreement her rights are protected and she has an avenue for raising concerns.

All surrogates also have the right to exercise their autonomy free from paternalism. That is why we would be reluctant to prohibit traditional surrogacy, which is medically safer for the surrogate. If the surrogate and the intended parents agree that traditional surrogacy is what they all want, then there is no principled justification for refusing them the option. Similarly, we respect the fact that some women would genuinely prefer unpaid surrogacy. If the regulatory processes are robust then the additional risks associated with both traditional and altruistic surrogacy should be much reduced. Again, there is no principled reason for refusing to register a woman who has a conscientious objection to payment.

It is important to emphasize that not all aspects of professional ethics apply to surrogacy. Surrogates have more freedom in some respects than members of the caring professions. For example, they are free to refuse their services even if this appears to conflict with anti-discrimination laws, while a professional is not. A surrogate's personal beliefs and values are allowed to influence her decision about entering an arrangement. To see why, it is helpful to consider the difference between a registered nurse and a registered surrogate. A registered nurse makes a commitment to care for any patient she is assigned in the course of her employment without discrimination. There are a few instances in which she can profess a conscientious objection to carrying out a procedure, but they are very limited and the wide range of areas in which to nurse provides scope to avoid those situations. The nurse's duties are generated by her employment and professional obligations. The surrogate, by contrast, has no duty to offer her services at all, as we showed in Chap. 3. Her registration does not impose a duty to be a surrogate *per se*. Rather, it confirms that she is a suitable person to act as a surrogate. She has no duties to anyone until she enters a surrogacy arrangement.

Surrogacy is not a profession. A woman is perfectly free to refuse to act as a surrogate on any grounds at all. This is how it should be given the nature of the relationship between intended parents and surrogate. They all need to be comfortable with each other and to be treated with respect and consideration. If, in the extremely unlikely situation that a surrogate agreed to act for a gay couple even though she personally disapproved of gay couples having children, it would be difficult and stressful for them to have her carrying their baby. At the counselling stage of the process, if not before, such a fundamental disagreement over values would quickly be discovered. Proceeding with the relationship would be ill-advised unless the circumstances were particularly compelling.

The Intended Baby's Rights and Interests

Certainty for the intended parents by way of legal parentage from birth also provides certainty for the intended baby. Looking at surrogacy through the UN Convention on the Rights of the Child (1990), Paula Gerber and Katie O'Byrne (2015) identify the child's rights to an identity, name, nationality, and to know and be cared for by its parents as central to surrogacy. The professional model provides for all of these rights from birth, without the need for a transfer of parentage or any dispute about who the child's parents are.

Children also have the right to family relations and this causes some of the complications in current regulatory frameworks due to a perceived difficulty over determining who the family is. However, we think there is a clear path through the thicket. There is already an established practice of registering donors in ART so that the child's right to know its genetic identity can be upheld. And while children born through donor-assisted reproduction may have the right to know who their biological parents are, much more would need to be done to show they had the right to a relationship with them. A similar provision should hold for gestational origins. Accepting that children born through surrogacy have a right to know their genetic identity does not mean that they must have a relationship with their biological parents. The child also has a right to know how it came into the world and who carried it. That does not mean a relationship has to be established or maintained. The right to know one's genetic and gestational origins is relatively easily satisfied with record-keeping (Gerber and O'Byrne 2015: 94).

The child has the same rights regardless of whether the intended parents use domestic or transnational surrogacy and in this matter the best interests test is entirely appropriate. Legal barriers to recognizing surrogacy arrangements are indefensible, given that they can lead to a child being left parentless and/or stateless. Legal prohibition does not stop people using transnational surrogacy; it merely ensures that they do it dangerously. Rather than wait for a Hague Convention, reforms must be undertaken at a state level to protect the children's basic rights regardless of what penalties are imposed on the parents. If a child's interests really are paramount, then that imposes obligations on the country it finds itself in through no fault of its own.

Over and above basic rights, the intended baby has interests that impose moral obligations on the surrogate and the intended parents. It has an interest in being born healthy, which means that the surrogate's gestational care must be to a high standard and her approach to pregnancy intelligent and evidence-based. Pregnant women are bombarded with advice and recommended diets. They are told of hazards to the fetus that have no evidential base and they may be reluctant to do things that are quite safe because of misinformation on the internet—the contemporary repository of 'old wives' tales'. The surrogate, with the support of the various professionals involved in the arrangement, has to be able to filter out the nonsense, including when it comes from the intended parents. She has to be able to think critically about her own beliefs about pregnancy and discard those that are false or dangerous.

Abortion for Fetal Abnormality

In some tragic cases the intended baby has an interest in not being born at all. Severe fetal abnormalities include conditions that impose such a burden of suffering on a child that its quality of life is negative. Not all disabilities or conditions would meet that threshold. These conditions are relatively rare and consist of only those where no amount of love or care can compensate for the pain and suffering the child undergoes. All other conditions fall into the category of cases where reasonable people can disagree over whether a termination is in the child's interests or not. However, because there are situations where the intended baby has an interest in not being born, the surrogate cannot have a conscientious objection to abortion *per se*. If she did then the intended baby would potentially have a legitimate interest that could not, in principle, be met.

It could be the case that the intended parents have a conscientious objection to abortion under any circumstances. If they do, then that would have to be respected, in that it should not preclude them from using surrogacy. However, it could not bind the surrogate as this is one of the points at which the intended baby's interests could diverge from those of the intended parents. Because all parties have to be able to live with the outcome, it is crucial that appropriate professional support is available at all times. A woman cannot be forced to have a termination and she cannot be prevented from exercising a legal right to terminate a pregnancy. The decision rests with the surrogate and it has to be voluntary. She must be able to make decisions on ethically relevant grounds, which are the intended baby's interests. (However, we allow one important exception, which we discuss in Chap. 6.)

Screening Intended Parents

Once the baby is born, it has an interest in having adequate parents. That raises the question of screening the intended parents for suitability to parent. Both scholarly literature and practice embrace the spectrum from screening equivalent to that for adoptive parents to no screening at all because it would breach procreative privacy (Jacobs 2006). The professional model could apply with a range of statutory screening requirements, as long as these occurred prior to a pregnancy being established, but it could not work in an environment where there was no screening at all. This is because the intended baby's interests must be considered independently of those of the intended parents and the surrogate. For example, a criminal background check on the intended parents could be justified in order to exclude those whose behaviour constitutes a risk of harm to the child, such as convictions for child sex abuse, but excluding everyone with a criminal conviction of any kind would not be morally justified. Not all criminal behaviour poses a risk of harm to others, even children, and convictions acquired in youth may reflect only adolescent impulsiveness that is outgrown by the time someone needs a surrogate.

There could be other reasons for refusing surrogacy services to intended parents, although we suspect that the demanding nature of the professional approach would lead to a degree of self-selection. If the intended parents are not willing to accept their obligations to the surrogate, then they should not be accepted for treatment. That does not entirely eliminate the risk of trouble occurring during the relationship but when things go wrong there are services to support the parents and surrogate so that relationship breakdown and the devastating consequences that arise in current frameworks can be avoided. The surrogate cannot withhold the child and the intended parents cannot withhold payment or make unreasonable demands. Those features of the professional model cover the vast majority of the problems that do arise during surrogacy relationships.

The professional model cannot prevent all forms of unethical behaviour occurring. In spite of a rigorous selection process, the surrogate could still act against professional advice and put the intended baby at risk during the pregnancy. For example, she could use substances or miss clinic appointments. It would be tempting to apply financial penalties in such a situation but that would be a mistake. It would bring back one of the most troubling features of the commercial model in which the exercise of control over the surrogate's behaviour risks breaching her rights. A pregnant woman cannot be forced to attend clinic appointments, nor can she be compelled to follow dietary guidelines. The surrogate is a pregnant woman with the same rights she would have under any other circumstances.

All that can legitimately be done to reduce the risk of opportunistic behaviour by the surrogate has been done before the pregnancy is established. That is why the steps to ensure that surrogates are trustworthy are so important. She can, however, be deregistered so that she is unable to enter another surrogacy arrangement. Some women have two or three surrogate pregnancies so deregistration would have an effect, potentially limiting the number of babies put at risk, but it is important to realize that surrogacy, just like the caring professions on which it is modelled, can never be entirely safe. The professional model minimizes risk but we do not claim that it can eliminate it.

Regulatory Power

The professional model requires a robust legal framework to support the regulatory authority. The power to remove licenses from clinics and deregister surrogates for serious ethical breaches, and to set the rules for professional practice is a delegated one. The same is true for other self-regulating professions, such as medicine, law and psychology. Their decisions can be challenged in court and the court has the authority to uphold them or overturn them. For example, if a doctor is struck off the medical register and her appeal is turned down, she would be guilty of a criminal offence if she continued to practice as a doctor. The same structure has to be in place for the practice of surrogacy for the same reason, which is the prevention of harm.

That means, however, that the state has to have consistent policies and legislation that fully acknowledge the legitimacy of surrogacy.

Tolerance of the practice without legal enforcement—the situation in many jurisdictions—is almost as undesirable as an outright ban because when things go wrong there is no redress and people are at risk of serious harm. Because there is still some antipathy to the practice, the temptation to leave policy unchanged is understandable. However, there comes a point when social change has to be acknowledged or the people most affected by it are left with *de facto* discrimination against them even if they officially have equal rights. With surrogacy, we have reached that point.

It might be argued that having a register of surrogates could be off-putting for intended parents but the professional model envisages many routes to registration. These include family members or friends applying, online matches through surrogacy support sites and women who are interested in being a surrogate applying through the official website instead of through a support site. The selection of a registered surrogate need not be a chilling and clinical process as the clinics could model themselves on the best agencies in the US who provide profiles of the available surrogates in an appropriately personal way. It is still vitally important that intended parents and surrogates are a good match for each other on issues important to both of them. The relationship is an intimate one and potentially a continuing one if the intended parents hope to keep the surrogate in the child's life. Registration acts as a filter so that intended parents can be more confident that they can trust the person they choose to care for their intended baby.

Transnational Surrogacy

Clearly, domestic surrogacy would be easier to regulate than transnational surrogacy but we do not think that banning the use of transnational surrogacy is likely to be successful, nor do we think it is morally justified. Instead, we think that the reality of transnational surrogacy has to be acknowledged and citizens using it be guided to use it well. This suggests that states should take steps to accredit clinics in other jurisdictions where the practices are of an acceptable standard and that country is prepared to support such an arrangement. Children born through these clinics should be treated the same as children born through domestic surrogacy. If countries were prepared to do this, then many of the dangers to surrogates and the children could be significantly reduced. Intended parents could do the necessary paperwork at home, have the advice and support of their own country and face no difficulties bringing their child back with them. The child's rights would be protected. Unauthorized surrogacies could be subject to the sort of difficulty that all transnational surrogacies currently face, thus deterring people from using them. If a smooth, safe alternative were available, most intended parents, who are not seeking to do anything wrong, would use it. Their reasons for going abroad should be acknowledged as legitimate. The shortage of domestic surrogates and prohibitive costs are valid reasons for seeking a transnational surrogate. Those who pursue unauthorized transnational surrogacy would deserve more scrutiny. They might be precisely the ones who should be stopped.

Conclusion

Appropriate regulation of surrogacy is crucial to the safety of all parties. The main objective is to secure legal parentage for the intended parents. Courts variously use genetic relationship, gestation, best interests of the child and intention to assign parental rights. We argued that all but intention risk leading to counterproductive or harmful outcomes. In particular, surrogacy challenges gestation as a criterion for determining parentage because the surrogate who gestates the baby does not intend to be its legal mother. There is a widespread belief in the existence of maternal-fetal-attachment, but this is not supported by current research and obscures the nature of surrogacy relationships. An infant forms an attachment to its primary caregiver(s). There is no prior attachment or bond with the gestational mother.

We argued that the intended parents should be the legal parents from birth and that the surrogate should not be a legal mother at any point. The agreement entered into before a pregnancy is established is binding on both parties. The intended parents cannot refuse parental responsibility and the surrogate cannot acquire it. Once a pregnancy is underway it is too late for anyone to change their minds.

Surrogates would have extensive rights that include fair compensation that is not tied to particular conditions in the agreement. She retains all her rights as a pregnant woman and is entitled to care and support at all times, including after she has given birth. The confidential pre-registration process would protect women from being coerced into surrogacy because they could safely disclose the fact knowing that it would not be stated in the letter to the intended parents declining to register her. Regulation would be robust enough to accommodate a surrogate's conscientious objection to payment and also a triad's preference for traditional surrogacy, which is medically safer for the surrogate. All surrogacies would be regulated in order to ensure the protection of both intended parents and surrogates regardless of the type of surrogacy they have chosen.

The intended baby's interests are considered independently of the interests of the intended parents and the surrogate. Its primary interest is in being born healthy so the surrogate's gestational care would have to be guided by professional advice and evidence-based research. Normally, a surrogate with a conscientious objection to abortion would not be registered because in some tragic cases it is not in the interests of the intended baby to be born. Some screening of the intended parents' background would be necessary to avoid known risks of serious harm to the child but it would not be as extensive as that for adoptive parents.

The regulatory framework we have argued for provides protection to all parties in a surrogacy arrangement and removes a great deal of the uncertainty for intended parents and surrogates. Putting it into practice requires the skills of a range of professionals. We now examine these in detail.

References

Altenhofen, S., Clyman, R., Little, C., et al. (2013). Attachment security in three-year-olds who entered substitute care in infancy. *Infant Mental Health Journal, 34*(5), 435–445.

Bainham, A. (2008). Arguments about parentage. *Cambridge Law Journal, 67*(02), 322–351.

Chervenak, F. A., & McCullough, L. B. (2009). How should the obstetrician respond to surrogate pregnancy? *Ultrasound in Obstetrics and Gynecology, 33*(2), 131–132.

Crawshaw, M., Purewal, S., & van den Akker, O. (2013). Working at the margins: The views and experiences of court social workers on parental orders work in surrogacy arrangements. *British Journal of Social Work, 43*(6), 1225–1243.

Drabiak-Syed, K. (2011). Currents in contemporary bioethics: Waiving informed consent to prenatal screening and diagnosis? Problems with paradoxical negotiation in surrogacy contracts. *Journal of Law, Medicine & Ethics, 39*(3), 559–564.

Gerber, P., & O'Byrne, K. (2015). Souls in the house of tomorrow: The rights of children born via surrogacy. In P. Gerber & K. O'Byrne (Eds.), *Surrogacy, law and human rights* (pp. 81–112). Burlington: Ashgate.

Gheaus, A. (2012). The right to parent one's biological baby. *Journal of Political Philosophy, 20*(4), 432–455.

Gheaus A. (2016). The normative importance of pregnancy challenges surrogacy contracts. *Analize: Journal of Gender and Feminist Studies, 20*(6), 20–31.

Jacobs, M. B. (2006). Procreation through ART: Why the adoption process should not apply. *Capital University Law Review, 35*(2), 399–411.

Jacobson, H. (2016). *Labor of love: Gestational surrogacy and the work of making babies*. New Brunswick, NJ: Rutgers University Press.

Jenkins, J. M., McGowan, P., & Knafo-Noam, A. (2016). Parent–offspring transaction: Mechanisms and the value of within family designs. *Hormones and Behavior, 77*, 53–61.

Lorenceau, E. S., Mazzucca, L., Tisseron, S., & Pizitz, T. D. (2015). A cross-cultural study on surrogate mother's empathy and maternal–foetal attachment. *Women and Birth, 28*, 154–159.

Margalit, Y. (2014). In defense of surrogacy agreements: A modern contract law perspective. *William & Mary Journal of Women and the Law, 20*(2), 423–468.

Millbank, J. (2015). Rethinking 'commercial' surrogacy in Australia. *Journal of Bioethical Inquiry, 12*(3), 477–490.

Office of the United Nations High Commissioner for Human Rights (OHCHR). (1990) *Convention on the Rights of the Child*. Available at: http://www.ohchr.org/en/professionalinterest/pages/crc.aspx.

Porter, L. (2015). Gestation and parental rights: Why is good enough good enough? *Feminist Philosophy Quarterly, 1*(1), 1–27.

Redshaw, M., & Martin, C. (2013). Babies, 'bonding' and ideas about parental 'attachment'. *Journal of Reproductive and Infant Psychology, 31*(3), 219–221.

Schoenmaker, C., Juffer, F., van Ijzendoorn, M. H., et al. (2015). From maternal sensitivity in infancy to adult attachment representations: A longitudinal adoption study with secure base scripts. *Attachment & Human Development, 17*(3), 241–256.

Storrow, R. F. (2015). Surrogacy: American style. In P. Gerber & K. O'Byrne (Eds.), *Surrogacy, law and human rights* (pp. 193–216). Burlington: Ashgate.

Van den Dries, L., Juffer, F., van Ijzendoorn, M. H., & Bakermans-Kranenburg, M. J. (2009). Fostering security? A meta-analysis of attachment in adopted children. *Children and Youth Services Review, 31*(3), 410–421.

Van der Voort, A., Juffer, F., & Bakermans-Kranenburg, M. J. (2014). Sensitive parenting is the foundation for secure attachment relationships and positive social-emotional development of children. *Journal of Children's Services, 9*(2), 165–176.

Walsh, J. (2010). Definitions matter: If maternal–fetal relationships are not attachment, what are they? *Archives of Women's Mental Health, 13*(5), 449–451.

Walsh, J., Hepper, E. G., Bagge, S. R., et al. (2013). Maternal–fetal relationships and psychological health: Emerging research directions. *Journal of Reproductive & Infant Psychology, 31*(5), 490–499.

6

The Professions and Professional Ethics

Introduction

Surrogacy arrangements involve a range of professions all of whose members are bound by codes of ethics specifying their obligations to patients or clients. The surrogacy 'triad' (Rotabi et al. 2015: 578) of intended parents, surrogate and intended baby requires inclusive but discerning attention from each profession. It must be inclusive because all three members of the triad have rights and/or interests, but it must also be discerning because the obligations towards each member differ.

Under the professional model the involvement of the same set of professions—medical, nursing, midwifery, counselling, legal and social work—would be needed. However, the nature and, in some cases, the extent of their involvement would change. Importantly, their work would be supported by a regulatory framework that would significantly reduce the levels of uncertainty and inconsistency they now face, to the benefit of all concerned.

As is clear from Chap. 5, the role of legal professionals would change under the professional model. At the moment practitioners have to draw up contracts that might or might not be enforceable and protect

© The Author(s) 2017   **145**
R. Walker and L. van Zyl, *Towards a Professional Model of Surrogate Motherhood*,
DOI 10.1057/978-1-137-58658-2_6

their clients' interests in a process fraught with risk. They have to guide their clients through the inevitable court proceedings needed to effect parental transfer, which could be swift and uncomplicated or contentious and prolonged. The costs are significant. Under the professional model there is a standard agreement and no court involvement. The intended parents' and surrogate's solicitors are required only to draw up the relevant documents concerning power of attorney and guardianship in the event of either party being incapacitated and to provide general advice on their legal rights and responsibilities in surrogacy arrangements. Thus, both time and costs would be considerably reduced. Our focus in this chapter, therefore, is on the role of medical professionals, counsellors, social workers, and midwives and maternity services.

Medical Profession

For both intended parents and surrogate the medical profession plays a central role. Medical ethics centre on duties to the patient, whatever type of medicine it is. Surrogacy falls principally within the domain of fertility specialists. There are some ethical complexities for these specialists that are unique to surrogacy. In standard fertility treatments requiring ART, the patient in need of treatment and the person who intends to carry the pregnancy is the same person. Whether the woman requires donor sperm, donor eggs, or both, the specialists' obligations are principally to her. In surrogacy the intended mother is only ever a patient if her eggs are to be used and once that is accomplished she ceases to be a patient. The surrogate is the patient from the very beginning, with fertility specialists, to the end, with obstetrical care providers. The implications of her status as patient are profound and not always well understood by practitioners and regulators.

As we noted in Chap. 4, Israel's system does not fully recognize the surrogate as the patient. But even in more ethically rigorous settings the surrogate's rights are sometimes discounted. In a study of Canadian surrogacy Shir Dar et al. (2015: 347) report that the 'gestational carrier' has to stipulate

that she will provide the treating and attending physicians with all perti-
nent information required to keep the [intended parents] informed and
will waive relevant medical privilege she holds with respect to the procedure and the pregnancy.

Such a clause is disturbing because it fails to consider what it means for
the surrogate to have patient's rights. It is a form of commodification.

The surrogate is the only person directly affected by all aspects of
pregnancy and is no different from any other pregnant woman in that
regard. She has the right to self-determination and bodily integrity. She
also has the right to decide what level of physical risk she is prepared to
accept. These rights make pregnant women practically inviolate and their
informed consent obligatory in all matters concerning the pregnancy.
They cannot be asked to waive their right to informed consent and it
cannot be overridden. However much others might desire her to undergo
particular screening or intervention for the sake of the fetus, a pregnant
woman cannot be forced to do anything against her will without it being
a serious breach of her rights. The only time her consent can be overridden is in emergency care for herself and these cases are relatively rare.

In surrogacy, these rights require the medical professionals to disregard the interests of the intended parents who, under the professional
model, have no leverage to pressure the surrogate themselves. For example, they cannot threaten to refuse to take the child if she does not do
what they want. These threats have been effective and even supported
by contractual law in some US States (Drabiak-Syed 2011: 563). The
health professionals caring for the surrogate at any stage have only one
patient: her.

It might be relatively easy for intended parents to accept that they
cannot be involved in decision-making about the course of the pregnancy but it could well be more difficult for them to accept that they do
not have the right to information about the pregnancy either. Pregnancy
encompasses the most intimate aspects of a woman's body and how it
functions. Information about it is deeply personal and sensitive. A pregnant woman has the right to decide what, if anything, will be disclosed
and to whom. This applies in surrogacy as well and means that the

obstetric team has to have her consent before they give any information to the intended parents (Chervenak and McCullough 2009; Reilly 2007). Although information about a pregnancy concerns the fetus, in which the intended parents have a very strong interest, there is no way of turning that into a right to information without compromising the rights of the surrogate, which are more fundamental.

The professional model recognizes and plans for the tensions between the rights and interests of the parties. Surrogates are selected for their ethical qualities as well as medical and psychological fitness. The surrogate's sharing of information is an act of generosity. The professional model would look for generosity of spirit in the surrogate, but acts of generosity cannot be obligatory. Requiring the surrogate to share information would nullify the right to confidentiality. However, a surrogate with generosity of spirit will be discerning in her judgements about information sharing and respect the needs of the intended parents. She would still have the right to withhold information that she felt was too personal or sensitive to disclose but would be reluctant to withhold information without a good reason to do so. Sharing information is a response to the intended parents' vulnerability. So is including them in discussions about decisions that have to be made. Because there is professional support available to them all, the surrogate could have some confidence that difficulties in the relationship that arise through a disagreement or when something goes wrong during the pregnancy could be resolved without increasing her vulnerability. That would make it less risky to her personally to share information. The professional model supports openness without sacrificing the surrogate's rights. It provides her with grounds to trust that it is indeed safe to disclose information. This is why it could not support the system in Israel where the patient is the intended mother. The medical file is in her name and she receives test results, not the surrogate (Teman 2010: 121).

Embryo Transfer

However, the surrogate's rights also have important implications when fertility specialists are working to establish a pregnancy. Her right to bodily integrity requires them to protect her from infections the genetic parents might have. This means that the genetic parents have to permit intense and potentially intrusive scrutiny of their health status before any material is transferred. The risks largely centre on sexually transmitted infections and Hepatitis B or C (ASRM 2015).

A more complicated issue is that of embryo transfer itself. There is evidence of differential treatment of gestational surrogates compared with other IVF patients. They are more likely to have multiple births as a consequence of multiple embryo transfer, which is less common in other IVF patients where single embryo transfer (SET) is becoming standard practice (Wang et al. 2016; White 2016).

The prevalence of double embryo transfer (DET) is troubling and a concerted effort is being made in Europe, including the UK, to reduce its use. According to a consensus statement by the Association of Clinical Embryologists (2011: 151): 'Multiple births are the single biggest risk to the health and welfare of children born following fertility treatment.' There are also 'significant health risks' to the woman, including 'miscarriage, pre-eclampsia, haemorrhage and operative delivery' (Leese and Denton 2010: 28). However, a conflict of interest arises for fertility clinics because they are under pressure to maintain a high live birth rate, which is why they have been reluctant to adopt SET for all of their fertility patients (Scientific Advisory Committee 2011: 3). Although their duty to the patient calls for SET, the competition for patients favours DET. Patients themselves are influenced by the additional cost from more treatment cycles, the idea of completing their family if they have a twin pregnancy, and a preference for twins, even with impairments, over no pregnancy at all (Leese and Denton 2010).

The chances of establishing a pregnancy reduce with age and are also affected by the quality of the embryos (Roberts et al. 2011). However, SET with frozen embryo replacement in younger patients is now as successful as DET (Scientific Advisory Committee of the Royal College of Obstetricians and Gynaecologists 2011: 4). Given that surrogates will normally be under 35, the case for insisting on SET is strong unless there are compelling reasons to consider DET, such as poor quality embryos (Harbottle et al. 2015). It is likely to be as successful as DET and with a much lower risk of multiple pregnancy. It is unreasonable to impose the extra risk on the surrogate or the intended baby.

The cost of surrogacy motivates increased use of DET. However, the practice threatens the rights and interests of the surrogate and intended baby. As the success rate for SET improves, requests for DET should decline and those who still want it should be closely scrutinized as it suggests a lack of regard for the surrogate as a person. Transnational clinics that routinely transfer multiple embryos and then perform fetal reductions would not be accredited and are precisely the ones that should be targeted by legislation to close them down.

Clearly, good counselling and support is crucial to help the intended parents and surrogate work through the ramifications of the surrogate's status as patient and support them if and when distressing situations arise. We envisage the counselling profession playing a significant role in surrogacy under the professional model.

Counselling

Counsellors are already involved in surrogacy and treatment for infertility but, in some cases, their role is ill defined and there are genuine debates about how to use their services. For example, there is disagreement about whether counselling should be compulsory or voluntary and whether it should be included in the treatment fee or paid for independently (ESHRE 2001). The professional model enables us to shed some light on those issues.

Counselling has several different functions and it is important to keep these separate when advocating the use of counsellors in surrogacy. There is no generic form of counselling that is ready to apply indiscriminately. The European Society of Human Reproduction and Embryology's guidelines outline four distinct 'tasks' for which counselling can be used. These are: 'information gathering and analysis,' 'implications and decision-making counselling,' 'support counselling' and 'therapeutic counselling.' That they have a role in fertility treatment and, by extension, surrogacy is well established. The first two tasks are carried out before the treatment begins. They enable the couple (and surrogate) to understand all the options available to them and work through the implications of those options before they commit to a course of action. Support and therapeutic counselling are available during treatment and after treatment. The distinct types of counselling help us see where and how counselling should be deployed in the surrogacy process. In some cases there are models of good practice that would not change, particularly in the early stages while the intended parents are exploring their options. It is important, however, not to use counsellors as gatekeepers to services.

Each step in the surrogacy process is quite separate. It is important not to conflate them as that causes ethical problems for the professionals. Specifically, it creates a dual role for counsellors. In one role their duty is to screen intended parents for suitability to parent, while in the other their duty is to support them as they work through the ramifications of choosing surrogacy. The latter task requires client candour, while the former encourages client self-censorship. Professional codes of ethics normally direct counsellors to avoid dual roles. The pre-registration screening of the surrogate should be administered by the regulatory body using their own preferred professionals with the appropriate training and expertise. Once a surrogate has been registered, counselling for the intended parents and surrogate enables them to assess all the information and what it would mean for them to undertake the process. The counsellor works with them as they decide whether surrogacy and, specifically, this surrogacy relationship is what they all really want. That is quite different from a process that determines whether they will be approved for surrogacy. In the former they can be open and candid because the counsellor has obligations only to them as clients. Because the counsellor is not there to decide whether they may have the surrogacy service, they are under no pressure to say the 'right' things. They also have confidentiality. The counsellor has just one role, which is to help them decide for themselves whether (this) surrogacy is the right thing for them.

While we think that counselling for this step should be obligatory we also think that their decision to proceed should be respected and accepted. Effective counselling will enable them to explore all the implications for them and, if they are prepared to proceed, their autonomous decision should stand. Any concerns over whether they should be allowed to use surrogacy must be addressed earlier.

Once the intended parents and surrogate have made a decision to proceed, the counsellor's task shifts to 'support counselling' and their availability throughout is essential. However, the use of counselling should be voluntary. Clinic staff might strongly encourage the intended parents and/or surrogate to use the counselling services but cannot mandate it.

The intended parents would have to bear the cost of counselling for all of them one way or another. There are two ethically significant advantages to including a set amount for counselling as part of the treatment fee. First, the medical staff can recommend counselling without any incentive to do so. There is neither a real nor apparent conflict of interest. Second, support counselling is there for clients 'experiencing distress' so an additional fee at that point puts up a barrier that could prevent the intended parents from acting in their own best interests. With the cost of surrogacy already high, they could be strongly tempted to forgo the benefit of counselling if they had to pay another significant sum of money. That could lead to unnecessary distress and difficulties in the relationship that could have been avoided. If it is the case that difficulties in the surrogacy relationship arise from inadequate professional support then it is essential that relevant support is accessible at all times and that there are no real or perceived conflicts of interest for the professionals providing it.

One potential conflict of interest remains in fertility treatment counselling. While the clinic team might be keen to see couples continue with treatment and view counselling as serving that end, the counsellors have a duty to the patients to explore the possibility of discontinuing treatment (Norré and Wischmann 2011). We do not think that a conflict of interest is inevitable. Medical ethics require that fertility specialists treat patients only while it is in their interests to continue and only with their consent. A counsellor's role is to help patients assess for themselves whether they do in fact wish to continue. This is particularly important in surrogacy where the intended parents and surrogate might have different views.

All staff have a duty to provide routine psychosocial care, which addresses the emotional wellbeing of the patients but is not an attempt at counselling, for which they are not trained (ESHRE 2015). Carol Wilson and Brenda Leese (2013) think that fertility nurses are particularly well placed to provide emotional support because they are involved with the patients at so many stages of the process. They make the same claim for midwives, which we support, but that raises a question about the continuity of care when the fertility treatment ends and obstetric management begins.

Support counselling has to be continuously available and if fertility clinics' role ends with an established pregnancy there is a risk that counselling provision ends as well or that it transfers to a new counselling team. It seems clear that it is in the interests of the intended parents and the surrogate to have continuous service provision. The only reason for changing to new counsellors would be that the surrogate and/or the intended parents wanted to.

Therapeutic counselling is needed if psychological problems occur. In most surrogacy relationships these do not arise but it must be remembered that success rates in IVF are still low enough that intended parents and surrogates face disappointment, distress and worse on a sadly frequent basis. The value of a continuing, trusted support service with referrals to more highly specialized practitioners is very high for those who do not experience a good outcome.

Social Workers

If counsellors should not be gatekeepers then several questions arise. Should there be any gatekeepers and, if so, who should they be? If they are determining who may and may not avail themselves of surrogacy, what criteria should they apply? When should this screening take place?

It is fair to say that there is a considerable degree of uncertainty at the moment. Every jurisdiction where surrogacy is legal has its own practices, some more principle based than others. Some scholars are concerned that screening breaches procreative privacy to an extent that would not be acceptable for other parents, including other users of

ART (Jacobs 2006). Others think that at least some intended parents should undergo screening equivalent to that for adoption (Botterell and McLeod 2016). Social workers frequently have the task of assessing the intended parents at some point, with little guidance on how to do it and within a judicial framework that is not fit for purpose (Crawshaw et al. 2013). In New Zealand, for example, the intended parents have to adopt their baby under an Act passed in 1955, no earlier than 12 days after it is born and following a social worker's evaluation of them as adoptive parents. In the UK evaluation can be up to 6 months after the baby has been placed with the intended parents. Judges have been granting parental orders well after the statutory 6-month limit, even when the intended parents are clearly in breach of the law regarding 'reasonable expenses' because the baby's interests are paramount (Horsey 2016). But the Parental Order Reporters (PORs), who are appointed by the court to do the evaluations, are not the only ones facing confusion as a result of the framework in which they must function.

Fertility clinics in the UK are required to make some form of child welfare assessment before agreeing to provide treatment. The evaluation of a couple as potential parents to a future child is obviously difficult and that is before privacy concerns are considered. When the list provided by the Human Fertilisation and Embryology Authority (HFEA) is examined, the intrusive nature of the assessment becomes clear. Each criterion is either almost impossible to assess, or is an invasion of privacy that no other potential parents have to tolerate, or both. For example, the clinic is supposed to determine whether 'there is a risk of significant harm or neglect to that child or any other child', whether there is 'violence or serious discord in the family', 'mental or physical conditions', 'drug or alcohol abuse', or 'heritable medical conditions' that would impair the ability to care for a child (Hale 2014: 28–29). Some of the considerations are clearly relevant to child welfare and easy to evaluate, such as 'previous convictions relating to harming children' and 'child protection measures' (Hale 2014: 28). But if the clinics strictly adhered to the rules, the number of patients treated would plummet because, while they are to proceed with 'the presumption that parenting will be supportive' they also 'should refuse treatment if... they cannot obtain enough information to conclude that there is no significant risk' (Hale 2014: 29). Even if clinics employed social workers, it would be a near hopeless task.

PORs, who are appointed only when the intended parents apply for a parental order, come into the process for the first time after the baby is born. They are required to determine whether 'reasonable expenses' only have been paid to the surrogate and make a child welfare assessment, but the parlous state of the regulations means that they have to use their own discretion on what to evaluate. This leads to wide variation between PORs (Crawshaw et al. 2013). They also know that the judge will probably grant the order, regardless of their findings, because it is almost never in the child's best interests to be removed from the intended parents.

Nevertheless, Satvinder Purewal et al. (2012) report that overall, PORs usually enjoy their work and tend to have a positive view of surrogacy. They would like to see better regulation, more accurate birth registration documents, and better preparation for the intended parents. We endorse all of these. However, nearly half of the participants, which is nearly half of the total number of PORs in the UK, expressed high role ambiguity and these participants were far less positive about all aspects of surrogacy. The researchers worry that these 'individual biases' could flow into their reports and recommendations to the court. If they did, it could have 'grave consequences' (Purewal et al. 2012: 98). It means that, in the UK, intended parents have an almost 50% chance of encountering a POR who is unclear about his or her role and has a more negative attitude to surrogacy.

The primary concern of the social work profession is protection, and the scope of their practice includes the whole triad (Rotabi et al. 2015). Lack of research and inadequate regulation leaves the profession struggling to determine how to carry out that role. It is not their normal type of child protection work, nor is it social justice and the protection from exploitation of vulnerable women (Rotabi et al. 2015).

Screening of the intended parents for their suitability to parent should occur prior to the agreement being signed. Treatment would not begin until the approval was in place. It is too late to be doing it once a pregnancy has been established. Only social workers with specialist training in fertility and surrogacy should undertake it, for the same reason that fertility counselling is a specialist field. General social work and counselling training do not equip practitioners for those roles and they can do real harm. Surrogacy is not a form of adoption and the application of the principles underlying adoptive placements are unhelpful at best and harmful at worst.

The crucial difference between adoption and surrogacy is the obvious one. Adoption applies to a child who already exists and in surrogacy the decisions are made before a child has even been conceived. Social workers know a lot about the children who will need adoptive parents. Their characteristics vary according to age and the circumstances under which they become available but there is extensive research to draw on when they are assessing whether potential parents will be good parents. Not everyone who might make a good parent would make a good adoptive parent. To evaluate adoptive parents from a child welfare perspective is to ask either 'will these people be good parents for this child?' or 'will these people be good parents for children with these specific needs?' Those are difficult questions to answer but they are more straightforward than the one in surrogacy, which is 'will these people make good parents?' Sheryl de Lacey et al. (2015) conducted a study of counsellors in New Zealand and Australia who had to apply the child welfare principle in ART. They report that counsellors find the principle meaningful but very difficult to apply. It is often seen as 'impractical' and 'slippery'. Their problems are increased because their role is not clearly defined. Their responsibility is to do an assessment of the physical and mental health of their patients, and not to assess what sort of parents they would make (except insofar as the risks to their health would affect it), but neither counsellors nor their patients found it easy to keep the two tasks separate. The counsellors' main problem, though, is that the patients are not parents yet and there is no child to parent. That is what makes the principles of child welfare difficult, though not impossible, to apply.

We think there is a much better question to ask when screening intended parents as parents: 'is there a compelling reason why these people should not be parents?' It is logically the first question that should be asked because if the answer is 'yes' then the process goes no further. It is also a question that shifts the burden of proof onto the regulators. The intended parents would not have to prove that they would be fit parents, a virtually impossible task due to lack of objective evidence. The state has to prove that they would not. The evidence for that would exist in the form of background information that is all that could legitimately be used to justify a 'no'. This is where questions about prior convictions, previous involvement with child protection services or officially documented concerns about violence should be asked and can yield useful information. The procreative liberty rights of the intended parents would be better protected under such a system because the grounds for claiming that a person is unfit to parent are very stringent and a case has to be put forward that the intended parents could rebut. They would have the right to appeal the decision, which could be done through the family court system. For the vast majority of intended parents that initial screening step would be brief and inexpensive. It would also allow social services to allocate the scarce resource of social workers to more important priorities such as the protection of children at risk and the placement of actual children available for adoption.

The last step is the delivery of the intended baby.

Midwives and Maternity Services

Only a pregnant woman has the right to determine how the labour and delivery of the baby will be managed. She chooses her midwife or obstetrician, the place she will give birth and the level of intervention she is prepared to accept during a normal delivery. The role of the professionals is to inform and advise rather than to dictate and control. These rights are deeply embedded in the relevant codes of ethics. A common source of ethical problems for practitioners is a woman's preference for something that will compromise her safety or that of the baby. However, in surrogacy an additional layer of complexity appears at two points. The first is when the intended parents disagree with the decisions the surrogate makes because they may put the intended baby at higher risk than they are prepared to accept. The second is after the delivery when the midwives have two sets of patients instead of one. The intended parents are now the parents and entitled to all the services that would be provided to other parents of a newborn. The surrogate is entitled to all the post-delivery care mothers receive pertaining to themselves rather than the baby.

We think the first of these problems is far less likely to occur under the professional model because the surrogate herself is responsible for ensuring that the intended baby's interests are served. She has provided gestational care throughout the pregnancy on these grounds and continues to do so until the baby is safely delivered. As the intended baby's principal interests are to be born alive and, preferably, healthy, she is unlikely to choose a course of action that would put personal preferences above the baby's welfare. Her ability to act on professional advice in delivery is just as important as acting on it during the pregnancy. Conversely, her duty to the intended baby would require her not to act on ill-informed preferences of the intended parents.

The second type of problem requires practitioners to adjust their practice to accommodate surrogate births. Some delivery units already do this very well. The surrogate receives all the care she needs and the intended parents are treated as any other parents, with a room if that is the custom and staff teaching them how to manage a new baby. There are many different ways for the units to adapt. If it is the practice for midwives to provide continuing care for the first weeks of the baby's life, then the parents might have their own while the one who delivered the baby continues to care for the surrogate. If the professionals involved at this stage have a positive view of surrogacy then there is no reason for services to struggle with the new reality.

However, difficulties do arise when the triad has to use professional services whose members do not see surrogacy as a legitimate way to form a family and do not attempt to accommodate it. For example, after delivery the staff may treat the surrogate as the mother, excluding the parents and ignoring the protestations of the surrogate that she is not the mother and that all information should go to the parents not her. In such situations the families face the same negativity that some LGBT families do when they use maternity services. Same-sex couples using surrogacy are particularly at risk of discrimination.

Many of the staff behaviours that lesbian mothers, in particular, experience also occur in surrogacy. For instance, in the exclusion alluded to above, 'non birth-mothers were not accepted as genuine or legitimate parents and were essentially prevented from participating in various health-related procedures.' They often experience 'inappropriate questioning' and 'refusal of services' (Hayman et al. 2013: 122–123). Sometimes it is worse: 'lack of sensitivity and respect', 'disparaging comments' and the use of 'common stereotypes', which tend to be negative, have all been reported (Dahl et al. 2013: 676). The forms they have to fill in do not accommodate the reality of their relationships, rendering the co-mother 'invisible' (Dahl et al. 2013: 678). The impact of marginalization should not be underestimated. For surrogates and intended parents who face exclusion, inappropriate questions, such as 'did you have sex with the father?' disapproval for 'giving away your baby' and 'taking another woman's baby', the effect is just as harmful. Pregnancy and childbirth is a stressful time that is also meant to be joyful. When staff fail to show acceptance and inclusion, the experience can be permanently tainted. Heteronormativity is not the only bias in maternity services. All maternity service providers have a duty of care to all their patients. Prejudice against non-traditional families exercising their legal and moral rights is unethical and unprofessional. Respectful treatment should not be a matter of luck.

The Surrogate

One of the unique features of the professional model is the requirement that the surrogate have specific ethical qualities analogous to those expected of professionals. Currently, the behavioural expectations of the surrogate have to be specified in the contract or agreement and all are potentially negotiable. They are individual items and tend to be inflexible, which makes them inadequate for unexpected eventualities. They leave too much power in the wrong hands. The intended parents should not have the power to control the surrogate's behaviour with financial conditions and the surrogate should not have the power to withhold the baby from them.

Throughout this book we have emphasized the ethical qualities from which right conduct should flow: trustworthiness, generosity and care.

All are personal qualities that underpin good professional conduct. They are the best hope for ensuring that, in an uncertain enterprise, the surrogate will carry out her duties to the intended baby, her principal concern, and the intended parents. The surrogate has to be able to recognize what is required at any particular moment and do it, whether it is care or generosity and whether the situation is routine or unexpected. She has to have good judgement because there is no list of instructions that could possibly cover all that might happen. She has to be able to understand and apply professional advice. That is a stringent demand because we know that patients often do not understand the information they are given or cannot accurately evaluate risk. For example, attempts to make SET standard practice meet resistance because many patients think, often erroneously, that establishing a twin pregnancy is a good outcome (Roberts et al. 2011).

The professional model also protects surrogates from unreasonable demands. Professionals in general have rights as well as duties, with regulatory bodies that enable them to refuse to do things that would breach their code of ethics or that would put them at undue risk. In surrogacy this provision not only protects the surrogate's rights, it also extends to her duty of care to the intended baby. The intended parents cannot insist that she do things that are against the interests of the intended baby. DET would be against the interests of both the surrogate and the intended baby and she should not even be asked to consider it.

During the pregnancy itself, the surrogate will take professional advice as her principal source of guidance and ignore requests from the intended parents that run counter to it. There are many routine practices where disagreement could occur. For example, if the surrogate is pregnant during the influenza season she will be advised to be immunized against it. At whatever time she is pregnant, she will be advised to be vaccinated against whooping cough (pertussis). Influenza puts the intended baby at risk but also the pregnant woman. The intended baby has a significant interest in being born with some immunity to whooping cough, because infants cannot be vaccinated before the age of 6 weeks and it is prevalent enough in many countries that babies are dying of it. In New Zealand, immunization for both seasonal influenza and whooping cough is provided free to pregnant women (Ministry of Health 2016). Even if the intended parents are opposed to vaccination, the surrogate should not decline it. But we also have to consider the surrogate's own beliefs and how these might affect the intended baby.

Most professions are able to allow for conscientious objection to carrying out certain tasks as long as the practitioner makes a referral to someone who will do it. It is not without controversy, but patients or clients will not be forced to go without the service if an individual is unable to provide it for religious or moral reasons. Unfortunately, surrogates are not in that position. They cannot refer the intended baby to someone else. That means the screening of surrogates must include a careful investigation of whether there are standard practices to which she would not consent and which have a material impact on the welfare of the intended baby. Immunization is one such practice. It would be grounds for declining to register the surrogate because vaccination is actually safe, the recommendation is uncontroversial within the medical profession and the risks to newborn babies without it are well known. Abortion is another matter.

Conscientious Objection to Abortion

Although we think that an objection to having a termination on any grounds at all is problematic because it can be in the intended baby's interests not to be born, there are reasons for permitting surrogates who are opposed to abortion to be registered. Unlike vaccination, which is minimally invasive, has a vanishingly small rate of adverse events and benefits both the pregnant woman and the intended baby, abortion is a significantly invasive procedure, has nontrivial risks, and has a net benefit to a woman only if her health or life is seriously at risk. It is not a standard practice in the way vaccination is and there is genuine disagreement inside and outside the medical profession about when it is morally acceptable to terminate a pregnancy. The intended parents have to be prepared to accept, regardless of their own beliefs, that a surrogate has the right to terminate a pregnancy whenever it is legally permissible to do so. Given the nature of surrogacy, it is unlikely that she would do so except in extreme circumstances. Surrogates prepared to use the threat as a weapon against the intended parents do exist in private arrangements without any screening or in agencies where screening is inadequate, but rigorous screening reduces that risk. Of more concern are cases where the intended parents and professionals think that termination is in the best interests of the intended baby, but the surrogate opposes it. Does this mean that all potential surrogates with a conscientious objection to abortion should be refused registration? We do not think so. We think that most potential surrogates with a conscientious objection to abortion should be refused registration but that a small number should be considered seriously. These are the surrogates for intended parents who themselves have a conscientious objection to abortion and who would not agree to a termination on the grounds of fetal abnormality if the intended mother was carrying the pregnancy herself.

The medical profession is already required to work with parents who have these beliefs and it has adapted to manage the consequences. For example, a decision to deliver a baby with severe abnormalities does not commit anyone to a decision to treat that baby if it is not in its interests to do so. Providing futile treatment is unethical and there are well-established procedures in many jurisdictions to facilitate withdrawal of treatment if the parents oppose that withdrawal. Once a baby is born it has rights that must be upheld even where the parents disagree with the doctors' assessment. The court is there to test the doctors' claims and those of the parents and decide what is in the best interests of the baby. These provisions are needed only rarely and are sometimes used to get consent to continue or begin treatment the parents oppose. In most cases, the parents can accept the assessment of the specialists and they can see for themselves the condition of the baby in front of them. Prior to birth everyone is limited in what they can determine from the scans and tests. A comprehensive assessment is only possible after the baby is delivered. If treatment is futile, which is not always easy to decide, then comfort care is given to the baby until it dies. It is an inherently distressing situation and no one should expect to feel happy about it, whether there is a termination or whether the baby is allowed to die, but some parents, at least, prefer to be holding their baby while it dies and know that they did not cause its death. This is a valid preference, which is why we think it reasonable for such parents to seek a surrogate who has the same values and beliefs in this regard and why it would be ethical to register her to act as their surrogate.

When it comes to delivery, the surrogate should not be permitted to have conscientious objections to interventions. An idealized desire for a natural birth with the intended parents present may have to give way to a much less natural delivery if the intended baby is at risk. These situations are common so it will be an important part of the screening of surrogates to ensure that they would not refuse the interventions professionals deem necessary to deliver the baby alive and healthy.

Conclusion

There are six professions involved in surrogacy under the professional model. Each has a specific role with duties to different members of the triad at different points of the process. They would provide fully integrated services to ensure that the relevant support and care was available throughout the process.

Social workers with specialist training would screen the intended parents for serious risk to a child before they entered an arrangement. That would normally be the extent of their involvement. The pre-registration process for the surrogate would be carried out by professionals appointed by the regulatory body who would not be involved in any subsequent surrogacy arrangement. This would prevent counsellors from finding themselves with a dual role, that is, as both gatekeeper and supporter.

Counsellors, also with specialist training, would guide the intended parents and surrogate through the decision-making process and then provide support counselling if they proceed.

Staff at the fertility clinic would have to adapt their normal practice in order to protect the surrogate's rights to confidentiality and to make decisions about the pregnancy. They would also be expected to refuse to transfer more than one embryo because of the risks to the surrogate. While patients often put pressure on clinics to transfer two embryos, the risk of adverse events is so high it could not be justified in a surrogacy. The surrogate would be put at risk with no benefits accruing to her.

Midwives and maternity services would have to make a significant adjustment to their practice because care for the surrogate is not care for the mother of the baby. When the baby is born the intended parents should receive all the services to which the parents are entitled, while the surrogate receives all the services to which a woman who has just given birth is entitled.

In all the professions involved with surrogacy an attitude change is necessary. Intended parents and surrogates currently experience a variety of responses to their arrangement. It is a matter of luck whether they are accepted or judged. The professionals have an obligation to treat all their patients with respect. Under our model, every professional involved in surrogacy has a distinctive and limited set of responsibilities. If they were allowed to fulfil their obligations without being burdened by conflicting roles, tasks outside their expertise or an uncertain legal framework, surrogacy would be much safer than it is now. To illustrate how the professional model would improve the current environment, we devote the final chapter of this book to a discussion of two well-known cases where the participants unwittingly placed themselves and their babies at risk.

References

Association of Clinical Embryologists, British Fertility Society and Royal College of Nursing. (2011). Multiple births from fertility treatment in the UK: A consensus statement. *Human Fertility, 14*(3), 151–153.

Botterell, A., & McLeod, C. (2016). Licensing parents in international contract pregnancies. *Journal of Applied Philosophy, 33*(2), 178–196.

Chervenak, F. A., & McCullough, L. B. (2009). How should the obstetrician respond to surrogate pregnancy? *Ultrasound in Obstetrics and Gynecology, 33*(2), 131–132.

Crawshaw, M., Purewal, S., & van den Akker, O. (2013). Working at the margins: The views and experiences of court social workers on parental orders work in surrogacy arrangements. *British Journal of Social Work, 43*(6), 1225–1243.

Dahl, B., Margrethe Fylkesnes, A., Sørlie, V., & Malterud, K. (2013). Lesbian women's experiences with healthcare providers in the birthing context: A meta-ethnography. *Midwifery, 29*(6), 674–681.

Dar, S., Lazer, T., Swanson, S., et al. (2015). Assisted reproduction involving gestational surrogacy: An analysis of the medical, psychosocial and legal issues: Experience from a large surrogacy program. *Human Reproduction, 30*(2), 345–352.

de Lacey, S. L., Peterson, K., & McMillan, J. (2015). Child interests in assisted reproductive technology: How is the welfare principle applied in practice? *Human Reproduction, 30*(3), 616–624.

Drabiak-Syed, K. (2011). Currents in contemporary bioethics: Waiving informed consent to prenatal screening and diagnosis? Problems with paradoxical negotiation in surrogacy contracts. *Journal of Law, Medicine & Ethics, 39*(3), 559–564.

European Society of Human Reproduction and Embryology. (2001). *Guidelines for counselling in infertility: Special interest group 'psychology and counselling'.* Belgium: ESHRE. https://www.eshre.eu/Specialty-groups/Special-Interest-Groups/Psychology-Counselling/Archive/Guidelines.aspx.

European Society of Human Reproduction and Embryology. (2015). *Routine psychosocial care in infertility and medically assisted reproduction—a guide for fertility staff.* Belgium: ESHRE.

Hale, B. (2014). New families and the welfare of children. *Journal of Social Welfare and Family Law, 36*(1), 26–35.

Harbottle, S., Hughes, C., Cutting, R., et al. (2015). Elective single embryo transfer: An update to UK best practice guidelines. *Human Fertility, 18*(3), 165–183.

Hayman, B., Wilkes, L., Halcomb, E. J., & Jackson, D. (2013). Marginalised mothers: Lesbian women negotiating heteronormative healthcare services. *Contemporary Nurse: A Journal for the Australian Nursing Profession, 44*(1), 120–127.

Horsey, K. (2016). Fraying at the edges: UK surrogacy law in 2015. *Medical Law Review, 24*(4), 608-621.

Jacobs, M. B. (2006). Procreation through ART: Why the adoption process should not apply. *Capital University Law Review, 35*(2), 399–411.

Leese, B., & Denton, J. (2010). Attitudes towards single embryo transfer, twin and higher order pregnancies in patients undergoing infertility treatment: A review. *Human Fertility, 13*(1), 28–34.

Ministry of Health. (2016). *Immunisation for pregnant women.* Wellington: Ministry of Health. http://www.health.govt.nz/your-health/healthy-living/

immunisation/immunisation-pregnant-women?gclid=CIukk8K7rs8CFYKa vAodIUsCrw.

Norré, J., & Wischmann, T. (2011). The position of the fertility counsellor in a fertility team: A critical appraisal. *Human Fertility, 14*(3), 154–159.

Practice Committee of the American Society for Reproductive Medicine and Practice Committee of the Society for Assisted Reproductive Technology. (2015). Recommendations for practices utilizing gestational carriers: A committee opinion. *Fertility and Sterility, 103*(1), e1–e8.

Purewal, S., Crawshaw, M., & van den Akker, O. (2012). Completing the surrogate motherhood process: Parental order reporters' attitudes towards surrogacy arrangements, role ambiguity and role conflict. *Human Fertility, 15*(2), 94–99.

Reilly, D. R. (2007). Surrogate pregnancy: A guide for Canadian prenatal health care providers. *Canadian Medical Association Journal, 176*(4), 483–485.

Roberts, S. A., McGowan, L., Vail, A., & Brison, D. R. (2011). The use of single embryo transfer to reduce the incidence of twins: Implications and questions for practice from the "towardSET?" project. *Human Fertility, 14*(2), 89–96.

Rotabi, K. S., Bromfield, N. F., & Fronek, P. (2015). International private law to regulate commercial global surrogacy practices: Just what are social work's practical policy recommendations? *International Social Work, 58*(4), 575–581.

Scientific Advisory Committee of the Royal College of Obstetricians and Gynaecologists. (2011). Multiple pregnancy following assisted reproduction. *Human Fertility, 14*(1), 3–7.

Teman, E. (2010). *Birthing a mother: The surrogate body and the pregnant self.* Berkeley: University of California Press.

Wang, A. Y., Dill, S. K., Bowman, M., & Sullivan, E. A. (2016). Gestational surrogacy in Australia 2004–2011: Treatment, pregnancy and birth outcomes. *Australian and New Zealand Journal of Obstetrics and Gynaecology, 56*(3), 255–259.

White, P. M. (2016). Hidden from view: Canadian gestational surrogacy practices and outcomes, 2001–2012. *Reproductive Health Matters, 24*(47), 205–217.

Wilson, C., & Leese, B. (2013). Do nurses and midwives have a role in promoting the well-being of patients during their fertility journey? A review of the literature. *Human Fertility, 16*(1), 2–7.

7

Hard Cases

Introduction

The case of Baby M is so famous that it could be said to belong to the folklore of surrogacy. It is often taken to show that surrogacy is immoral, and harmful to women and children. The case became the defining event for modern attitudes to surrogacy and created a difficult legacy for both intended parents and surrogates. However, as we will show, it looks very different through the lens of the professional model.

The Baby Gammy story, in turn, threatens to be the defining event for attitudes to transnational surrogacy, with consequences potentially even more detrimental to future intended parents, surrogates and the children born of these arrangements.

Hard Cases Make Bad Law: Baby M Revisited

The old adage that 'hard cases make bad law' is nowhere more applicable than in the case of Baby M. In 1985, when William and Betsy Stern sought a surrogate through an infertility agency in New Jersey,

© The Author(s) 2017
R. Walker and L. van Zyl, *Towards a Professional Model of Surrogate Motherhood*,
DOI 10.1057/978-1-137-58658-2_7

traditional surrogacy arrangements were informal but not illegal. As long as a baby was not being sold, the law had no interest in the practice. Betsy Stern had multiple sclerosis and thought a pregnancy might exacerbate her condition. She was criticized in the press for this decision but it was a reasonable one at the time because very little was known about the effects of pregnancy and childbirth on the condition. Current advice is that pregnancy is normally safe (National Multiple Sclerosis Society 2016). Stern also faced criticism for her desire to become a mother, even though multiple sclerosis does not necessarily impair a woman's ability to parent.

Mary Beth Whitehead was recruited by the Infertility Agency of New York in March 1984 and was selected by the Sterns in February 1985. Rudimentary screening for suitability included a psychologist's report that raised concerns about her ability to relinquish the baby and recommendations for further counselling before she committed to the process (Salkin 1999). These were disregarded by the agency. Whitehead agreed to act as a surrogate for the Sterns, for which she would be paid US$10,000. She was artificially inseminated with William's sperm and gave birth to a baby girl.

Whitehead found that she could not give away the baby and a legal nightmare began for all parties. Initially the lower court held that the contract was enforceable, awarded the Sterns parental rights and terminated Whitehead's. This decision was overturned on appeal, on the grounds that a contract cannot alter the legal status of a child's birth mother. Commercial surrogacy was held to be baby selling. The matter was finally deemed to be a custody dispute between the baby's mother, Whitehead, and father, William Stern. Betsy Stern had no status. William Stern was awarded custody but Mary Beth was granted visitation rights. Custody was given to Stern because it was deemed to be in the child's best interests.

Unless one assumes that it is always in a child's best interests to maintain a relationship with its biological mother, it is less plausible to think that Baby M would benefit from being required to spend time with Whitehead and her family. It should have been clear from her previous behaviour, which included going on the run with a newborn baby, that she would not be a good influence and was not stable.

The Sterns had named the baby Melissa but Whitehead, who had named her Sara, refused to use the name and compromised with 'Sassy'. We know this because she talked to the media (Salkin 1999). She told the press that, when she grew up, Sassy would be angry with the Sterns for what they had done. She vilified Betsy Stern. The Sterns had to take out an injunction to prevent her from publishing recent photographs of Melissa, whose privacy they protected fiercely. She wrote a book, which she called *A Mother's Story: The Truth about the Baby M Case* (1989).

When Melissa turned 18, she terminated Mary Beth Whitehead's parental rights so that Betsy Stern could adopt her. In 2007 she said of the Sterns 'I love my family very much and am very happy to be with them. I'm very happy I ended up with them. I love them, they're my best friends in the whole world, and that's all I have to say about it.' (Kelly 2012) She wrote a Master's thesis at King's College London on the social impact of surrogacy. As of 2012, her parents were still married and living in the same place, Melissa was married and working as a medical writer in London and Whitehead could not remember the last time she saw her.

The response to this case, which had worldwide media coverage, forced legislators and policy makers into making decisions that have come to be a blight on contemporary practice. Some states outlawed all surrogacy arrangements and others banned commercial surrogacy. Traditional surrogacy, where the surrogate is the biological mother of the child, as Whitehead was, has been shunned. With the advent of IVF, genetics and gestation could be separated and gestational surrogacy became the norm. Mary Beth Whitehead became the poster child for the dangers of traditional surrogacy because she showed that a 'natural' mother would never be able to give up her child. Her very obvious psychological problems have also been used as evidence that women who are prepared to be surrogates must be abnormal in some way. In spite of rapidly accumulating evidence that the type of surrogacy makes no difference to the outcome and that surrogates do not experience long-term difficulties (Imrie and Jadva 2014; Jadva et al. 2015), the voices of those who seek to do something so 'unnatural' are rarely heard. The case of Baby M is routinely cited but very little is made of the end of the story. Melissa grew up. And as soon as she was able to, she legalized the truth: the Sterns are, and always were, her parents. Melissa's own views are confirmed by another action she took. She asked the judge who had originally upheld the contract, and given the Sterns parental rights, to perform her wedding ceremony. The courts and commentators today should bear in mind the outcome of this most notorious early case of surrogacy.

Would the professional model have led to a better outcome? Yes. Mary Beth Whitehead would not have been registered as a surrogate. The rigorous screening the professional model requires would have prevented that. Even at the time it was clear that Mary Beth Whitehead was not a suitable candidate for surrogacy. Yet in the course of this saga, however much she brought the trouble on herself by her actions, she suffered a great deal. Everything she did led her away from her desire, which was to have a relationship with the child she had given birth to and whom she regarded as her child the same way she did her other genetic children. It was quite clear, also, that this was a one-way attachment and not a relational bond. Melissa was securely attached to her primary caregivers, the Sterns. She did not need a relationship with her genetic mother. This illustrates the findings of the research into infant attachment and the gestational bond that the pregnant woman may develop. Infant attachment is to the primary caregivers who, as far as Melissa was concerned, were Betsy and William.

It is difficult to tell whether the genetic link made a difference to Whitehead's ability to relinquish the baby or not. There was no alternative to traditional surrogacy at the time. However, with the evidence we now have that traditional surrogacies do not lead to more problems with relinquishment, it is plausible that she would have had a struggle regardless of whether she was a traditional surrogate or a gestational one. Either way, she would not have been accepted for surrogacy under our model and, to be completely fair to current practices, she would not make the grade at any reputable agency. She would have been spared a great deal of suffering had her interests and welfare been taken seriously, as they would be in the professional model.

Betsy Stern, too, would have been accorded respect and status as the intended mother. She was effectively edited out of the story. She was not the baby's mother by anyone's reckoning even though she was the social mother from the time William was granted custody. Apart from being a target of opprobrium, she was invisible until her daughter quietly put the record right. Under the professional model, Melissa would have been Melissa Stern from the moment she was born. William and Betsy would have been recorded as her parents on the birth certificate and the surrogate's name would have appeared somewhere on the document as the genetic and birth mother but not as one of the legal parents.

It is essential that the surrogate be emotionally stable for her own welfare as much as for that of the intended parents and the intended baby. However, it is also crucial that she conducts herself ethically. Problems did not emerge in the course of Mary Beth's pregnancy and we can be confident that her gestational care was good. However, once she found that she could not relinquish the baby she appears to have had no ability to separate her own interests from those of Melissa. For example, while the Sterns guarded Melissa's privacy, Whitehead was still talking to the media when Melissa was 13 years old. Her refusal to use the name that the Sterns had given the baby was also a denial of Melissa's own emerging identity. She was angry with the Sterns but seems not to have considered the effect of her vitriolic public outbursts about Betsy on Melissa nor been able to consider the possibility that her own feelings would not also be those of the child. She could not accept Melissa's love of and attachment to the Sterns. She could not accept that Melissa had rights and interests that differed from her own. She failed in the duty of care to Melissa that arose from her role as a surrogate. In the complete absence of professional support for her after the surrogacy, we do not find this surprising. The case shows just how unsuitable the contractual model is, given that the only way of resolving crises is through the adversarial court system.

Under the professional model, help would be provided to any surrogate who was struggling with relinquishment. The one option that is not available to her is to seek custody of the child. That is made abundantly clear from the outset and would prevent women from engaging in a futile course of action that could only harm the people at the centre of it. The risk of such an outcome is remote but is one of the main reasons why the process of screening and then counselling to work through all the ramifications of a decision to enter a surrogacy agreement must be so rigorous and painstaking. Once a baby is on the way it is too late to undo the decision, because a change of mind on anyone's part is so detrimental to the intended baby's interests as well as those of the party that did not change its mind. In this respect all the adults are held to their commitments.

The legal framework under which this particular dispute was settled did not change the actual nature of the arrangement and the ethical duties that arose from it. More often than not, and thanks in part to the Baby M case, the laws do not reflect the nature and ethical status of the relationship. Amidst all the noise generated by feminists and conservatives rallying to Mary Beth's cause, there was very little attention given to Melissa's interests as an independent being.

The professional model can only mitigate the risk of relationship breakdown between surrogate and intended parents and it cannot exclude the possibility of an unsuitable surrogate slipping through to the detriment of all parties, including the surrogate. We must emphasize that, except in cases of fraud where a surrogate sets out to deceive the intended parents, a woman who becomes a surrogate with good intentions but without the necessary psychological resilience is also harmed by the experience if things go wrong. We do not seek just to protect intended parents and the intended baby.

The media reports and much subsequent scholarly literature portrayed Mary Beth Whitehead as a poor woman who was exploited by a rich couple who wanted her to give up her baby for money. When she refused to give up the baby and also refused the money she was considered even more of a victim. The facts seem to us to be different. If Mary Beth was exploited or a victim, the Sterns were not the perpetrators. The agency should never have permitted her to be a surrogate. The Sterns were also victims of the agency because they trusted the surrogate selected from its books. When so little was known about surrogacy the worst they could be accused of is naivety. They then found themselves in a court system that was completely unprepared for the case and forced it into a framework that denied the reality of the situation. The person who bore the cost of this was Melissa. The Sterns did all they could to protect her but the court's ruling prevented them from protecting her from the one thing that put her at most risk: an alleged non-custodial parent who had a right to visitation and also appears to have had every intention of poisoning the child against her parents. In this respect Melissa faced all the consequences that children of bitter custody disputes face but she had an additional burden. Unlike custody disputes where a relationship has broken down, her biological mother was not her mother. Furthermore, Mary Beth was able to pursue her campaign through the ever hungry media that could not get enough of the Baby M case. Only a court injunction, taken out by the Sterns when the child was two years old, prevented the publication of photographs that would have made her easily identifiable, and thus at risk of harassment as she went about daily life.

The case had a disproportionate impact on regulation and the future of surrogacy. The assumption that a woman cannot decide in advance whether she will be able to relinquish her baby was firmly entrenched to the detriment of two generations of surrogates and intended parents. The evidence is very clear that Mary Beth's difficulty was unusual but it has become the norm by which everything else is evaluated. The stigma associated with commercial surrogacy is, to this day, having consequences. Where surrogacy is permitted, the preference is for unpaid surrogacy arrangements, which, as we have shown, are exploitative. It also contributes to the shortage of domestic surrogates and the subsequent development of transnational surrogacy. Finally, traditional surrogacy has been prohibited in many jurisdictions and is avoided by intended parents anyway because of the mistaken belief that it is more difficult to give up a baby that is genetically yours. This increases costs to everyone and also puts the surrogate's health at greater risk.

Bad Law Makes Hard Cases: Baby Gammy and Baby Pipah

In 2016 the courts still let down the children of surrogacy arrangements. In our second case the media again play a significant role and mislead as to the facts. Again the case is given worldwide attention and the public forms erroneous judgments of the participants. There is a 'good' surrogate and 'bad' parents. There is the additional ingredient of a transnational surrogacy arrangement with a genuinely poor woman. Again, the actions of an agency create the conditions for a potentially tragic outcome. And again, the court is unable to reflect the reality of the arrangement because of the legal framework in which it must operate. But in this case, the intended parents contributed to their predicament. In an unusual move, the judge in the custody case ordered his judgement to be published in full and we have used it as the source for all the facts we present [Farnell & Anor and Chanbua (2016)].

In 2013, after 10 cycles of IVF, Australian couple David Farnell and his wife Wenyu Li, decided to try surrogacy as a last resort to have a child together. David had adult children from his first marriage. Because commercial surrogacy is illegal in Australia they went to Thailand. They had seen a documentary that presented surrogacy as a 'win-win' situation. It lifted Thai women out of poverty, which perhaps they should not have been so ready to believe. And it gave desperate couples the family they longed for. They used an agency, Thailand Surrogacy, which claimed to pay their surrogates more than others did. Having been advised not to use Wenyu's ova they used eggs from an anonymous donor and David's sperm. However, they claimed to their family and, later, the court, that they had used Wenyu's eggs (9).

The surrogate, referred to as Mrs. Chanbua throughout the court documents because of her name change after the events, 'found herself in debt' and applied to be a surrogate. She was told that she was too young so she 'assumed the identity of an older relative using fake papers' (9). On 23 May 2013 two embryos were transferred to her and she became pregnant with twins. It was clearly unethical to transfer two embryos to a young woman who had children of her own. The consequences were almost fatal for both babies. In late September the Farnells were told that there was a risk that one of the fetuses had Down syndrome and in late October this was confirmed to them. The male fetus was affected. What happened next remains in dispute but Mrs. Chanbua understood that the Farnells wanted her to abort the male fetus. This was emphatically denied by the Farnells and the agency's employee, Joy, who was involved in the case. At most the options were discussed and, in fact, by the time the diagnosis was confirmed it was too late for an abortion. The Farnells were angry that testing had not been done earlier.

Mrs. Chanbua had decided she wanted to keep the boy herself because, as the Judge put it, she 'had fallen love with the twins.' She had also been 'told by a fortune teller that the boy would bring good luck' (10). Although the Farnells continued to prepare for the birth of twins they were probably aware by this stage of Mrs. Chanbua's intentions. The twins were born prematurely on 23 December and the Farnells were still in Australia. They arrived on 29 December but were unable to see the babies without Mrs. Chanbua's permission. Both the babies were seriously ill in intensive care, but in a different hospital from that agreed with the Farnells. They had asked for the twins to be born at Bangkok Christian Hospital, which had expertise in Down syndrome. Mrs. Chanbua had, by this time, returned to her home town. The Farnells saw the twins the following day. The baby boy was at that hospital for 5 months before being transferred to another one.

The Farnells paid the same attention to both twins and bought nappies and milk for both of them. They met Mrs. Chanbua a total of six times and were only given the surrogacy agreement to sign on 3 January 2014. On 10 January David emailed his daughter to tell her that they had had to say goodbye to their little boy and left her with the clear impression that the baby had either died or was about to. It was a deception the Farnells continued when they returned to Australia. What had happened, however, was that they almost certainly learned at this time that they would not be allowed to take him.

Mrs. Chanbua was responsible for the twins' birth certificates. She registered the baby girl with the name 'Pipah' and handed over the certificate. She did not register the baby boy with the name his parents had chosen, 'Noah', but with the name 'Gammy', which fitted the pattern of her own children's names. She did not hand over his certificate. The Farnells received Pipah's certificate with a translation on 14 January. In spite of their request, it did not have her surname as Farnell nor her father as David Farnell. They asked Joy to 'plead with Mrs. Chanbua for them to have both children' (12) and visited Gammy until they left the country on 13 February.

Mrs. Chanbua did cooperate over Pipah's citizenship but this cooperation included omitting to mention the existence of Gammy. The Farnells kept quiet about Gammy, fearing that they would not be allowed to leave with Pipah either, if the truth was known. By this time Mrs. Chanbua was threatening to keep both babies and go to the police. Her lie about her age and identity possibly rendered the entire arrangement illegal and Antonio, the owner of the agency, contributed to their rising alarm by urging them to move hotels so that Mrs. Chanbua could not find them. The email from Antonio on 7 February was the last time they were able to contact him while they were there. To add to the stress, civil unrest was growing. Pipah's papers were processed immediately, her passport was available on 11 February and her parents were told of a travel warning advising foreign nationals to leave as soon as possible. They arrived home on 13 February, traumatized and fearing that Pipah could be taken from them. They had been the victims of Mrs. Chanbua's opportunism. Given the temptation to betray their trust in pursuit of her own interests she had done exactly that.

Sometime in March they tried to change Pipah's family name but were advised that this could not be done without the birth mother's consent. Their next attempt to 'regularise' Pipah's status was an application to the family court for a 'parental responsibility' order and 'permission to change Pipah's family name.' Unfortunately, they persisted with the claim that Wenyu's eggs had been used and, as this was a formal deposition, they committed perjury.

The worst aspect of their case was revealed in May when someone notified the Department for Child Protection and Family Support (DCP) that David Farnell had a child living at his address. David Farnell was a convicted sex offender and had been sentenced to 3 years in prison for 22 offences against young girls. He was released from prison in 1999 and following that there was, and is at the time of writing, no evidence that he has reoffended. He fully complied with the treatment programme he was offered and had the support of his family when he was released. Wenyu knew only that he had been in prison and learned of the nature of the charges when the story went into the public domain. Significantly, the DCP did not act on the information. It did not have David on its database of offenders who pose a risk to children and it had higher priorities for its limited resources.

In August the story of David and Wenyu Farnell's alleged abandonment of Gammy and David's criminal history became public in a media storm. Mrs. Chanbua's version of events became the orthodox account. The DCP began to investigate but did not allow the publicity and anger in the community to affect its risk assessment. Pipah was not removed but David had to move out for 6 weeks while the investigation was being conducted. He was then able to return home, a safety plan was put in place and an immense amount of support and scrutiny became their normal mode of life. And then, in April 2015, Mrs. Chanbua applied for custody of Pipah. By this time Pipah was 15 months old and past the age when she would find it relatively easy to attach securely to a new caregiver.

The principle for determining who raised Pipah was her best interests and welfare. The judge emphasized that there were only two options available to him, which were to leave Pipah with the Farnells to whom she was securely attached or return her to Thailand to live with her birth mother and twin brother (17). He was also severely constrained by the limits of the legislation, which did not permit him to give legal parentage to the Farnells. In fact, Pipah could not be deemed a 'child of a marriage'. In a classic example of the capriciousness with which genetic relationships are treated, under the Artificial Conception Act (1985), David Farnell was merely a sperm donor and as such 'is "conclusively presumed not to have caused the pregnancy" and is expressly declared not to be the father' (54). The father of the twins is Mr Chanbua because he was in a *de facto* relationship with Mrs. Chanbua, the legal mother of the children, at the time and had consented to the procedure (54). David Farnell is the only one who is genetically related to the children.

At the same time the DCP applied for a protection order, though of the lowest level, supervision, should Pipah remain with the Farnells. The judge decided that she would stay with them and said:

> While it is a matter of grave concern to leave any child in the home of
> a convicted sex offender, I have accepted the expert evidence that while

there is a low risk of harm if Pipah stays in that home, there is a high risk of harm if she were removed (17).

He declined to make the protection order because the DCP was already able to remain involved with the case as long as they saw fit and the provisions for Pipah's safety were very thorough. The expert evidence was that the Farnells were very good parents and that Pipah was Wenyu's highest priority. She had come to have a good understanding of the need to protect the child as well as how to do so. The wider family were providing support and had loving relationships with Pipah who was thriving in the environment. The whole family appears to be part of the safety network the Farnells are required to have and show a strong commitment to it. David never offended against his own daughter and this was an important consideration for the experts assessing the risk he might pose to Pipah. The Farnells were subject to a degree of scrutiny that went far beyond what other at-risk families might expect and the orders the judge made ensure that scrutiny will never be far away.

The Farnells were awarded equal parenting responsibility and an order to change Pipah's family name to Farnell was granted. It was deemed to be in her best interests to have the same name as the people who were raising her. However, on her registration documents the Chanbuas have to appear as her parents and the registrar could only be invited to consider adding information about the legal authority that gave the Farnells parenting responsibility.

The judge had a very negative view of commercial surrogacy but there is no evidence in the judgement that his disapproval made any difference to the orders he made. He was possibly a little inclined to let Mrs. Chanbua off lightly when it came to her dishonesty, but even if she had been held to the same expectations as the Farnells, the outcome would not have been different. The Farnells could not have been granted any more than they received and she could not have been granted any less because legally she and her husband are the parents and the Farnells are not.

The ramifications of the legal fiction are considerable and will affect Pipah's entire childhood. The judge made a determination of her best interests within the law as it stands and was clearly right to leave her with her family rather than send her to Thailand to the care of complete strangers with a different culture and language from the one that is already part of her identity. The psychologist's evidence made that quite plain. But the law does not recognize all of her interests and prevents anyone from acting to advance them.

The safety plan and indefinite involvement of the DCP are not issues that arise from the fact that Pipah is a child born through surrogacy. Given David Farnell's record, any child that he and Wenyu had would be subject to similar concern. It is worth noting, however, that it is very demanding. Pipah is not to be alone with her father and he is never to provide intimate care. She has to have a 'Words and Pictures' story read to her by a member of the safety network or one of her parents (and we use the term deliberately) in the presence of a member of the safety network every 3 months until the DCP and network agree it is no longer necessary. This story explains her father's past and why she must not be alone with him. It should be an evolving document suitable for her developmental stage. Her parents have to allow any professional providing care to Pipah to share information with other professionals and the DCP. The Farnells have to continue seeing their psychologists or other approved therapists (they each have one) until the DCP thinks it is not necessary. These professionals are also to be authorized to share information with the DCP. David has to have annual risk assessments until Pipah is twelve or the DCP thinks they are no longer necessary. Both Wenyu and Pipah can, and in Pipah's case will, be directed to complete an approved Protective Behaviours Program.

It is true that none of this would be necessary if the Farnells had not sought a surrogate but it is also true that had one of the IVF cycles worked, the child born to them would also have been subject to protection. The identity of the person who notified the DCP is confidential but it is reasonable to assume that that person, or someone else, would have notified the DCP had they been aware of any other child living with the Farnells. David Farnell returned to his community and kept his own name so his record is no secret to those living in the vicinity.

No other child would have been subject to some of the orders the judge made. The story Pipah is told has to include information about her origins in Thailand and the existence of her twin brother.

She obviously ought to be taught about her twin, although a truthful explanation about why he does not live with her is not going to redound to Mrs. Chanbua's credit. When she begins kindergarten and school the Farnells have to send Mrs. Chanbua samples of her artwork. The request for photographs was rejected on the grounds that Mrs. Chanbua has already gone against her lawyer's advice and published photographs of Gammy with an interview. She cannot be trusted to respect Pipah's privacy. The Farnells, on the other hand, are very protective of it.

The judge said 'Pipah's full ethnicity is unknown, but she clearly has a connection to Thailand in that her birth mother is Thai and she was born in Thailand' (105). That is true and we agree that all children born of surrogacy are entitled to know their origins. That includes where they were born and who their surrogate mothers were. However, we do not think that anything about the child's way of life need follow from this information. Many children are born in countries other than the ones they grow up in. It adds a little exotic flavour to their lives but they participate in the cultural life of their own country. Any additions to that are an optional extra. There is no compulsion for parents to raise their children to be bilingual for example, although it can have many advantages for the child's future. It is up to the parents to choose the best course for their children's upbringing. Unfortunately, the judge did not see things that way when it came to Pipah. It is not clear whether the egg donor was Thai, although it has been reported that she was (Van Wichelen 2016). Given that the judge said that Pipah's full ethnicity is unknown and that he rested his decisions on her birth place and the gestational mother's ethnicity we should not assume that Pipah has any genetic ties to Thailand. Nevertheless, the judge ordered that 'The Farnells shall engage Pipah in celebrating Buddhist festivals and events, including but not limited to, Visakha Bucha and Makha Bucha' (186). We also have no reason to believe that either of the Farnells are Buddhist. Even if they are, it is a breach of their freedom of religion and right to choose what cultural and religious experiences they want for Pipah. This breach is the result of bad law. Mrs. Chanbua has standing as Pipah's mother due to the perverse rulings required by dated and inappropriate legislation. That is the only reason why she has a say in how Pipah is brought up and that is why the judge feels free to intrude on her actual parents' autonomy and privacy. They might not want to celebrate those festivals or Pipah might not want to. Those are good enough reasons for anyone to opt out of any religious or cultural practice.

The invisible person in this case is Gammy. Mrs. Chanbua arranged for him to have Australian citizenship in the hope that Australia (but not the Farnells) would 'provide' for him if she was unable to do so. However, he is legally the child of two people who are not related to him and he has the name his surrogate mother chose for him, not that of the Farnells. Initially, Mrs. Chanbua may have believed that the Farnells did not want Gammy but she should quickly have been disabused of this notion. Joy urged her to give him to his parents at the time. They had clearly planned for the twins and accepted their son's Down syndrome. However, Mrs. Chanbua did not want to give him up and, because of the laws that prevail both in Thailand and Australia, she was able to keep him and intimidate the Farnells into not attempting to gain custody of him. We should not fall into the trap of seeing Mrs. Chanbua as a victim of exploitation. She was well paid, the Farnells sent extra funds to her after they returned to Australia (14) and arranged for better medical care for her during the pregnancy. The role of the agency in exploiting them should not be overlooked but Mrs. Chanbua succeeded in making them genuinely fear that she could keep Pipah as well if they made too much fuss about her having Gammy. They continued to believe they were unsafe when they returned to Australia. She might have been poor but she became a surrogate through a deliberate and sustained lie about her age and identity. She persisted in the story that the Farnells had abandoned Gammy even after she must have known it was not true. And it was very much worth her while to do so. Donations flooded in to support her while she raises Gammy. He has a trust fund that pays her a monthly amount and they live in a house provided by the trust. She is, or was, financially very much better off for keeping him.

It was never in Gammy's best interests for her to keep him. Down syndrome is a significant condition that causes developmental delays that require specialist education services. There are a number of associated health problems that need expert medical services. Parents require support services to assist them with raising a child with special needs. With the right care and support a child with Down syndrome can have a good quality of life and live well into adulthood, possibly able to work. Without them, their future can be bleak. Thailand struggles to provide health care to its population and provision of services for children with special needs is patchy. In Australia, Gammy would have access to everything he needs. In Thailand, even with the best of intentions, the Chanbuas cannot provide anything comparable. But they are his parents and that is where he stays. Photographs show a white child with the characteristic facial features of Down syndrome. He does not appear to share the ethnicity of the other children, which could be a problem for him as he grows older because he looks entirely different. At the time of the court judgement (April 2016) the information available to the judge was that he was well cared for and 'thriving'. The judge accepted the submission of the Human Rights Commission that 'it would be contrary to the human rights of both Pipah and Gammy to take into account any differences in the standard of living between the two households' (104). In other words, the fact that Pipah could be impoverished by the move to her birth mother's care would not be allowed to enter the calculation of her best interests. Concern about the effect of relative poverty on Gammy's welfare cannot be considered even though it will influence his life course in obvious and detrimental ways, even to the extent of how long he lives.

If media reports are to be believed, Gammy's life has taken an unfortunate turn. His mother is on the run from loan sharks and has not seen him for some months. He lives with her other children and their grandmother in the house provided by the charity. He is obviously securely attached to his family and during the interview was happy and active. But his grandmother says he sleeps in a cot with high wooden sides and if he was not in there she would get nothing done. The charity ensures that he lives in a good quality house and he is apparently receiving health care. His parents are moving to another town. This loan, for a truck for her husband's business, is the second since Gammy was born that his mother has taken out and not repaid. The first was a loan from the charity to start a small business, which failed because the interest proved crippling (Sainsbury 2016).

How would the professional model have helped? It might have prevented the twins being born. David and Wenyu would not have been approved for surrogacy because of his convictions. It would be impossible to stop them or any other couple from going to Thailand or other countries that provided surrogacy, legally or illegally. However, if compensated surrogacy were available in Australia, with only accredited transnational clinics as the alternative, a couple seeking citizenship and passports for children they could not legally account for would instantly alert the Embassy staff to potential child trafficking. States know what to do about that and the consequences for individuals involved are severe. The difficulty at the time was that the Thai international surrogacy industry was very poorly regulated but not explicitly illegal. Any jurisdiction in that position creates the conditions in which it is not clear to Embassy or immigration staff exactly what has led to the application. It could be trafficking, it could be a couple who thought that what they were doing was entirely legal and whose surrogacy was straightforward. It could be a couple in a serious predicament, such as the Farnells, with every incentive to suppress the facts. If it is clear whether the surrogacy is authorized or not then the staff at both Embassy and borders would know what to do because there would be a protocol. If it was approved at home and undertaken at an accredited clinic: issue the passport. If not, then investigate and take the appropriate steps. Ordinary surrogacy arrangements are not child trafficking any more than above board international adoptions are child trafficking. However, in both fields child trafficking is a risk. The welfare of all children who have been trafficked must be the highest priority. In surrogacy this might be more difficult to determine than in adoption because the children to be trafficked are created in the surrogacy arrangement. By contrast, intercountry adoptions involve children who have been illicitly removed from their birth family or who were genuinely in need of parents, but whose fate was to be placed with the wrong people. In either case the child's ethnicity is usually known and the place they come from is likely to be traceable. Kin might be available or other members of their community able to take them in. If they cannot be repatriated then better homes can be found for them. None of this is easy but it is achievable.

The crucial difference in surrogacy is that the children are born without pre-existing ties to the country. They are not usually related to the surrogate. They could have a genetic relationship with one or both of the intended parents or they could be donor offspring. The fact that they are born in one country rather than another is not necessarily relevant to welfare considerations. Pipah and Gammy could just as easily have been born in India or Ukraine. The connection is so tenuous that the only proper question to ask is 'what happens to them if we leave them here?' In India it can mean consignment to an institution and in Thailand it can mean the care of financially precarious individuals who would not be considered adequate adoptive parents. Yet that is in effect what the Chanbuas are. The answer to the question posed above could well be that they will have to be repatriated to the intended parents' country even if they do not remain in the care of the intended parents. The question for the authorities is whether the intended parents actually intend to parent and may have done things illegally or whether they are trafficking the children for abuse or exploitation. If they are sincere in their intent to parent, the next step is to determine their fitness to parent. Under the professional model, only those people without approval would come to the attention of the authorities and it would be appropriate to ask about their fitness to parent.

It would not do any harm for the richer states whose citizens cause the trouble to take more responsibility for the consequences. Current practices where states wash their hands of the problem and leave children stateless and parentless are inexcusable.

We join the judge in 'loathing' David Farnell's sexual offences. The couple's deceptions did call into question their credibility as witnesses. However, microscopic investigation of every aspect of their parenting shows that they are providing Pipah with a very good home in a loving and supportive family. Gammy could have had the same experience and would be receiving appropriate early education. To remove him from the Chanbuas now would be as psychologically harmful as removing Pipah would have been.

Rather than ban commercial surrogacy, the case shows just how urgent it is to provide safe, regulated surrogacy services with a clear plan for dealing with the cases of illegal surrogacy before it is too late to rescue the children. The Farnells could not go to Thai authorities for redress because the industry was unregulated. They were too afraid to tell the Australian Embassy about Gammy so could not even find out if they had any rights in the matter. They were on their own in a country where they knew nothing of the law, spoke not a word of the language and had every reason to be suspicious of the owner of the agency who quickly made himself uncontactable as the situation deteriorated. They were innocents abroad, believing what they had seen on television about 'win-win' transnational surrogacy. In that respect they were no different to thousands of other couples who have plunged into the dangerous world of commercial surrogacy in developing countries.

As a result of the public outcry over the 'abandoned' baby, Thailand banned international surrogacy, trapping hundreds of couples in the country while they negotiated a transitional process for permitting foreign nationals to leave with their babies. With Thailand and India effectively off limits, transnational surrogacy has shifted to Nepal. It will keep moving from state to state as long as bans rather than regulation are chosen as the means of control.

The Farnells were at the lower end of the spectrum of surrogacy arrangements that would not receive approval and will forever be regarded as the couple who abandoned their disabled child, in spite of the judge's explicit finding that they did not. Sadly, David Farnell will always be known as the paedophile who was allowed to keep his baby girl. Nothing he does now will remove that association from the public's mind. Pipah will grow up with that as people's first thoughts about her father.

The justification for approving intended parents who would not need approval for IVF does not rest entirely on the Farnells' unfortunate case. The vast majority of intended parents will keep their children safe, but the rare cases of child trafficking make it necessary to scrutinize all parents' backgrounds. This is because the potential harm to children is catastrophic. Where there is a low risk of catastrophic harm it is appropriate to apply the precautionary principle (Sunstein 2007). And there have been examples in Australia where children born from surrogacy have been sexually abused, including twins born to a Thai traditional surrogate (Back 2014) and a far graver case in which twins were procured through surrogacy solely in order to be abused (Bucci 2016).

If bans on transnational surrogacy in countries such as India and Thailand do push the practice underground, the only defence left for the children of illicit surrogacy arrangements is robust and well-regulated domestic and accredited transnational channels. The children born from such arrangements would be at no greater risk of harm than children born to any other parents. And children who arrived via other arrangements would be much easier to detect because their parents could not hide in the grey zone of irregular but not quite illegal transnational surrogacy.

Conclusion

The Sterns and the Farnells were the unfortunate victims of unregulated, dangerous forms of surrogacy. They fell into the hands of incompetent, if not corrupt, agencies and women who were not fit to be surrogates. Mary Beth Whitehead is a tragic figure. She did not set out to harm anyone and she herself suffered. Mrs. Chanbua was dishonest and unscrupulous in her quest to become a surrogate and in her subsequent behaviour. We have argued that many of the problems arise because of the laws that currently govern surrogacy, in particular the assignment of parental rights. The solution is not to ban surrogacy but to reform the law to ensure that it accurately and fairly represents the nature of the relationships.

In this book, we have set out the case for reform of surrogacy. Our professional model provides a new approach to surrogacy that addresses the legitimate concerns people have about the practice. The professional model has ethics at the heart of it and is grounded in robust regulation, which gives all parties certainty about parentage, ensures protection of their rights and interests, and provides appropriate professional support at all times. We believe it would make surrogacy a much safer method of family formation.

Intended parents and surrogates have obligations to each other and the intended baby that are profoundly ethical, yet the moral values expressed in the altruistic and commercial models of surrogacy are inappropriate given the nature of the relationship. However, the ethical principles and values of the caring professions, suitably adapted, do provide a sound basis for the ethical practice of surrogacy. Surrogates provide gestational care to the intended baby, which is why the analogy to the caring professions works. Once surrogacy is seen through this particular ethical lens, it is easier to see the weaknesses in current models that render the practice unsafe for all participants.

We argued that surrogacy is not inherently exploitative but that much of it is at present. Transnational surrogacy often both exploits and commodifies women, and intended parents from the developed world are frequently complicit. The lives of the impoverished women who gestate their babies are often not transformed by the money they earn as surrogates, in spite of what the clinics claim and the intended parents naively believe. Reforming transnational surrogacy requires the active intervention of richer states whose citizens use the services. However, if domestic surrogacy was properly regulated and legislation was updated, there could be fewer intended parents who look to transnational surrogacy. A merely tolerated practice with unenforceable agreements makes intended parents and surrogates very vulnerable, and puts the baby's interests at risk. It gives intended parents an incentive to go abroad where, ironically, they are even more at risk, especially when they try to bring the baby home.

The professional model has a theoretical foundation based on rigorous research in the social sciences. Anthropological research helped us see that the relationship between intended parents and surrogates is properly understood as a gift exchange. For a gift exchange to be satisfying there must be reciprocity, but in the altruistic model of surrogacy, this is forbidden. We identified generosity rather than altruism as the core moral value because it can be properly reciprocated. The appropriate response to generosity is gratitude.

The scholarly literature on trust shows why and how people make mistakes about whom to trust. These mistakes can have disastrous consequences in surrogacy. We demonstrated how professional trust, which has structures in place to reduce the risks associated with trusting strangers, can be adapted to surrogacy to provide a way to address these problems. It is important to bear in mind that surrogacy can never be entirely risk free. However, it can be made considerably safer than it is at present.

We have shown how the professional model would apply in practice. We have also demonstrated how it could have improved the outcomes in two almost notorious cases that have come to define perceptions of the practice. If policy and law reflected the facts about surrogacy instead of popular prejudice and beliefs based on discredited theories, most of the risk and all the uncertainty people face now could be eliminated or mitigated. That is why we think that surrogacy should become an established treatment for infertility, including social infertility, and a safe method of family formation for women with medical conditions that preclude pregnancy.

References

Back, A. (2014, September 2). Australian surrogate father allegedly abused twins from Thailand. *Sydney Morning Herald.* http://www.smh.com.au/world/australian-surrogate-father-allegedly-abused-twins-from-thailand-20140901-10b7m3.html.

Bucci, N. (2016, April 22). Man pleads guilty to sexually abusing his twin surrogate babies. *Sydney Morning Herald.* http://www.smh.com.au/national/man-pleads-guilty-to-sexually-abusing-his-twin-surrogate-babies-20160421-goc83m.html.

Farnell & Anor and Chanbua. [2016]. FCWA 17 (14 April 2016).

Imrie, S., & Jadva, V. (2014). The long-term experiences of surrogates: Relationships and contact with surrogacy families in genetic and gestational surrogacy arrangements. *Reproductive Biomedicine Online, 29*(4), 424–435.

Jadva, V., Imrie, S., & Golombok, S. (2015). Surrogate mothers 10 years on: A longitudinal study of psychological well-being and relationships with the parents and child. *Human Reproduction, 30*(2), 373–379.

Kelly, M. (2012, March 30). Kelly: 25 years after Baby M, surrogacy questions remain unanswered. *NorthJersey.com.* http://www.northjersey.com/news/kelly-25-years-after-baby-m-surrogacy-questions-remain-unanswered-1.745725?page=all.

National Multiple Sclerosis Society. (2016). *Pregnancy and reproductive issues.* http://www.nationalmssociety.org/Living-Well-With-MS/Family-and-Relationships/Pregnancy.

Sainsbury, M. (2016, September 25). New fears for Gammy: Loan sharks split family of Australia's abandoned surrogacy baby. *Sunday Herald Sun*. http://www.pressreader.com/australia/sunday-herald-sun/20160925/282471413340694.

Salkin, A. (1999, March 21). She's come a long way, baby M!: Gifted child born amid a two-family uproar thrives. *New York Post*. http://nypost.com/1999/03/21/shes-come-a-long-way-baby-m-gifted-child-born-amid-a-two-family-uproar-thrives/.

Sunstein, C. R. (2007). The catastrophic harm precautionary principle. *Issues in Legal Scholarship, 6*(3).

Van Wichelen, S. (2016). Postgenomics and biolegitimacy: Legitimation work in transnational surrogacy. *Australian Feminist Studies, 31*(88), 172–186.

Index

© The Editor(s) (if applicable) and The Author(s) 2017
R. Walker and L. van Zyl, *Towards a Professional Model of Surrogate Motherhood*,
DOI 10.1057/978-1-137-58658-2

The manufacturer's authorised representative in the EU is Springer
Nature Customer Service Centre GmbH, Europaplatz 3, 69115 Heidelberg,
Germany. If you have any concerns regarding our products, please
contact ProductSafety@springernature.com

Printed and bound by CPI Group (UK) Ltd, Croydon, CR0 4YY
23/04/2026
02095587-0002